THE WORD FOR EVERY SEASON

*Reflections on the
Lectionary Readings*

(CYCLE A)

Dianne Bergant, CSA

Paulist Press
New York/Mahwah, NJ

also in this series by Dianne Bergant, CSA
The Word for Every Season (Cycle B)
The Word for Every Season (Cycle C)

Cover design by Sharyn Banks
Book design by Lynn Else

Library of Congress Cataloging-in-Publication Data

Bergant, Dianne.
    The Word for every season : reflections on the lectionary readings (cycle A) / Dianne Bergant.
        p. cm.
    ISBN 978-0-8091-4673-4 (alk. paper)
    1. Church year meditations. 2. Bible—Meditations. 3. Catholic Church—Prayers and devotions. 4. Catholic Church. Lectionary for Mass (U.S.). Year A. I. Title.
    BX2170.C55B439 2010
    242´.3—dc22

2010007936

Published by Paulist Press
997 Macarthur Boulevard
Mahwah, New Jersey 07430

www.paulistpress.com

Printed and bound in the
United States of America

Contents

Introduction

The Catholic Bible Movement of the 1950s introduced us to what is known as the "historical-critical approach" to interpreting the Bible. This approach opened us to exciting new insights into the historical background of the stories with which we had become so familiar. What had often seemed baffling could now be better explained, and this without losing the religious mystery behind the biblical passage. Soon, even grade school children were devouring the fruits of this new method of interpretation.

Within the more recent past, we have gleaned new insights into biblical interpretation from various methods of literary criticism. This approach is not primarily interested in the concerns of the original author or the original biblical communities. It maintains that, once it leaves the original situation, the biblical text has a message in its own right, independent of the specific meaning of the author or the early communities.

This is similar to the case with music: One need not consult Bach to interpret one of his fugues. Everything needed for such an interpretation can be found in the score itself. So, everything needed for an interpretation of the Bible can be found within the Bible itself.

Over the years we have found that the employment of such interpretive approaches has enriched our understanding of the scriptures in ways too numerous to list. However, we maintain that the scriptures are more than religious texts meant to be studied with an eye to their importance to an ancient people, or as an example of well-crafted religious literature. We believe that the religious message that they contain is the foundation of our faith, and that somehow that religious message is meant to shape our own religious identity and to influence our behavior. We want to know what that message might mean for us today.

The reflections collected in this book are an attempt to address this final concern: What might that message mean for us today? These reflections spring from a careful examination of the lectionary readings for every Sunday and Solemnity of the liturgical year. Though at times historical or literary information might be offered, the focus here is on prayerful musing on the meaning that message might have for us today. It is in ways such as this that the word takes root in our hearts in and out of season.

Advent

FIRST SUNDAY OF ADVENT
Readings:
Isa 2:1–5; Ps 122:1–9;
Rom 13:11–14; Matt 24:37–44

WE ARE A PILGRIM PEOPLE

At Thanksgiving time, when people in the United States hear the word *pilgrim*, they immediately think of the Puritans, who were some of the earliest European settlers of this country. The words *pilgrim* and *Puritan* are often used interchangeably. However, the religious meaning of the word *pilgrim* is often better understood in other countries, where pilgrimage is more a religious practice than a matter of migration. Many people make pilgrimages to the shrine of Our Lady of Guadalupe in Mexico, or to Lourdes in France or Fatima in Portugal. In fact, we read in the Pastoral Constitution of the Second Vatican Council that we are a pilgrim people. Just what does this mean?

Pilgrimage is an apt characterization of the journey upon which we embark today. Liturgically, we begin the season of Advent. From this point of view, we are on a journey toward the feast of Christmas. On a much deeper theological level, we are beginning anew the journey to eschatological fulfillment. In other words, we are beginning our yearly reenactment of the drama of our salvation, beginning with the mystery of the incarnation (Christmas) and culminating in the celebration of Christ's ultimate victory (Christ the King). Today, we take our first steps on the way.

Our lifelong journey toward fulfillment is going to be a complicated and often tedious one and, lest we lose track of our ultimate destination, it is placed before us at the outset. In the first reading, the prophet Isaiah introduces the image of pilgrimage to describe the great gathering of the future. He announces that all nations will stream toward the mountain of the Lord, the place where God dwells. There they will all be instructed in the ways of

God, and in response they will "beat their swords into plowshares and their spears into pruning hooks; one nation shall not raise the sword against another, nor shall they train for war again." What a glorious image! What a poignant sentiment! What a timely promise!

The responsorial psalm is a joyous hymn that was meant to be sung as pilgrims journeyed to Jerusalem, the site of the Temple, and the dwelling place of God on earth. As we sing it today, it calls us to reflect on prominent aspects of this moving season. Liturgically, we are invited to look longingly toward Christmas, the feast that celebrates the incarnation of God among us. It would be a shame if children were the only ones who got excited about Christmas. Where along the way toward adulthood did we lose the thrill that should be ours at the thought that God has become one of us? Theologically, the psalm encourages us to set our sights on our own salvation and the salvation of our world, when Christ will bring to fulfillment the promise of ultimate peace.

When we turn to Paul's message to the Romans—and to us today as well—we are told what we must do to help bring about this vision of peace. He exhorts us: "Conduct yourselves properly." He warns us against "orgies and drunkenness…promiscuity and lust," lives of self-indulgence of any kind. More than that, he condemns the "rivalry and jealousy" that result in parish or family feuds and alienation, in ethnic or national antagonism and wars. If we are genuine pilgrims on the way to God's eschatological fulfillment, we must act as pilgrims, not as tourists. We must enter wholeheartedly into the pilgrimage, leaving behind whatever might hinder our progress, accepting whatever hardship our journey might entail.

The Gospel seems to paint a dire picture. It describes how the disaster of the flood caught the people of the time of Noah unawares, and it speaks of not knowing when the thief is coming during the night; it says that some will be taken and some will be left. Actually, the point of Jesus' teaching is that in each case the people were unprepared; the point is not the tragedy itself. Had they been prepared, there would have been no tragedy. It also presumes that had they known when the misfortune was going to occur, they would have been prepared. And that is the point! They did not know, and neither do we. And so Jesus admonishes us: Stay awake! Be prepared at all times! "For at an hour you do not expect, the Son of Man will come."

On this First Sunday of Advent, we set off on a pilgrimage to the fulfillment of God's promises and plans for our salvation, salvation from self-indulgence and disdain of others, salvation from small-mindedness and fear of life itself. We have before us a vision of universal peace and reconciliation among nations and religious bodies, among ethnic groups and families. Not too far down the road (Christmas), the Son of God himself will join us. There is great anticipation in our step; there is great urgency in our preparedness. This is the scenario placed before us today. It is up to us to decide whether or not we wish to join the pilgrimage.

Praying with Scripture

- What can you do to assure that weapons of war will be converted to implements of peace?

- Where in your life can you replace rivalry and jealousy with sentiments of kindness and understanding?

- How ready are you to meet God, not merely in death, but in life?

SECOND SUNDAY OF ADVENT
Readings:
*Isa 11:1–10; Ps 72:1–2, 7–8, 12–13, 17;
Rom 15:4–9; Matt 3:1–12*

THE PEACEABLE KINGDOM

The Peaceable Kingdom, a print by the German-born illustrator Fritz Eichenberg, has inspired many other artistic representations of this oft-quoted passage from Isaiah. In it, we see animals that are natural enemies sitting together peacefully under the widespread branches of a sheltering tree: a lion, a bear, a cheetah, a wolf, a snake, along with lambs, a rabbit, and a small child in their midst. When we consider the reality of the world of which we are a part, we might wonder: Is this scene merely a fanciful myth? An impossible dream? Or might it be a vision of our future, promised by God?

We sometimes forget that passages depicting such tranquility are really characterizations of future times, not actual descriptions of present reality. The future forms of the verbs tell us this. Isaiah envisions a future king who will be filled with the spirit of the LORD, and whose rule will establish peace. Perhaps in the prophet's day, Israel was enduring some political struggle or was threatened with invasion by enemies. In the face of acknowledged vulnerability and fear of attack, the prophet paints a picture of reconciliation and peace. Is this an example of denial, or of unrealistic optimism? On the contrary, Isaiah is reminding the people that the peace that they seek—that we all seek—is not impossible. It has been promised to us by God. That means that we must look to God, and not merely to our own human efforts, for this peace.

Paul's words to the Romans might well be addressed to us today: "Whatever was written previously [the passage from Isaiah] was written for your instruction, that by endurance and by the encouragement of the scriptures we might have hope." Hope for what? Surely more than merely hope for the coming of Christmas. We know that Advent is really the time set aside for us to remember that God is indeed "God-with-us." The conviction of God's presence in our midst is the grounding for the peace of which we speak at Christmas, the peace for which we all so earnestly yearn. Paul's exhortation is really quite simple: The harmony (peace) we seek is to be found in openness to others, the kind of openness we saw in Christ. He was open to both the Jews and the Gentiles. This openness, this hospitality will result in a peace that is perceptible.

This image of peace is radically different from what we normally consider peace to be. We might assume that we are at peace when we are not bothered by others. We might be able to secure such peace if we can control those others or the circumstances of our interaction with them. Or, we might not be bothered by them if we can distance ourselves from them. But this is certainly not the kind of peace envisioned by Isaiah, or the kind of social harmony preached by Paul, or the character of the reign of God proclaimed by John. In *The Peaceable Kingdom*, creatures that are natural enemies are at peace with one another.

If peace is of God, do we simply wait patiently for God to give it? By no means. The words of John the Baptist are loud and clear today: "Repent, for the kingdom of heaven is at hand!" This is the very message of the prophets of old. Like them, John called for a return to righteousness, to lives of integrity, to relationships rooted in honesty and respect. He spoke against presumption and arrogant reliance on one's religious origin, against complacency and shirking of responsibility, against disinterest in the welfare of others. John is the perfect herald of this message. His demeanor was as penitential as his message, but his attitude was self-effacing: "The one coming after me is mightier than I. I am not worthy to carry his sandals."

What does this repentance entail? The word *repent* comes from the Greek root for *metánoia*, a change of mind and heart, a change that is much more easily described than accomplished. The peaceable kingdom of God for which we long may require that we put an ax to resentments and biases that may be rooted in our hearts. We may have to winnow our greed and overindulgence; we may have to burn the chaff of our impatience. For sure, we will have to swallow our pride; we may have to refrain from demanding our rights and, instead, relinquish some of our importance. *Metánoia* means conversion from selfishness to genuine concern for others. And the image of the peaceable kingdom insists that these others are not merely those with whom we normally interact. Certainly peace must begin in our families. For it to be authentic, however, it must extend to those whom we might consider our natural enemies, either because of disposition, or because of gender, racial, ethnic, religious or economic background. If we want peace, we must change our hearts.

Praying with Scripture

- Pray for those whom you consider to be your enemies.

- Take steps to mend a broken relationship.

- Perform at least one explicit act of hospitality, welcoming others "as Christ welcomed you."

THIRD SUNDAY OF ADVENT
Readings:
Isa 35:1–6a, 10; Ps 146:6–10;
Jas 5:7–10; Matt 11:2–11

REJOICE IN THE LORD!

In the middle of Advent we pause for a moment of rejoicing. This is not so much a period of rest taken during a long journey; it is more like a short stop at a scenic view, where we stand in awe of the spectacular panorama before us. Advent is a liturgical journey toward Christmas, the feast that celebrates God's presence as one of us. The season is a preparation for the reenactment of our salvation, which begins with the incarnation and carries us through to eschatological fulfillment. Today, from our vantage point, we get a glimpse of that fulfillment. It is a scene of peace and healing. We know that when we meet the reality that we perceive now only from afar, we will be confronted by challenges and hardships. But today we are granted a preview of the fulfillment that lies in store for us.

Both the first reading and the gospel passage promise restoration and new life. In fact, scholars maintain that the gospel writer had the Isaian passage in mind when describing the fruits of Jesus' ministry. The people of God, both at the time of the prophet and during the early Christian period, believed that sin brought disorder into the world. This disorder manifested itself both in natural disasters and in human suffering. They also believed that God promised there would be a time in the future when the world would be put right again. This promise was the ground of their eschatological hope. Isaiah envisions this future time; Jesus claims it has already dawned, and he points to his deeds as evidence of it.

The poetry of Isaiah is strikingly beautiful. Only one who has witnessed barren land come to life can appreciate the prophet's depiction of the transformation of the parched desert and treeless steppe. Not only will nature be rejuvenated, but humans too will be restored to full life. The examples of people who suffer forms of physical impairment represent the entire human race, for we all are in some way impaired, and each of us longs for healing. These scenes of burgeoning life and restoration are harbingers of the time of fulfillment promised by God.

In the Gospel, before he launches into praise of John the Baptist, Jesus announces that the time of fulfillment is unfolding before the eyes of his hearers. He has inaugurated this long-awaited era; he has begun the restoration; the world is being transformed and human beings are experiencing the healing power of God.

I wonder how many of those who heard Jesus really believed his words. Did they realize that their world was being transformed before their eyes? But then, do we? Many of us think that our world is in decline. If we even believe that transformation will happen, we wait for God to accomplish it. We do not always realize that God works this transformation through us. We may not realize that we are like the farmers described in the Letter of James. They certainly must wait for God's gift of rain, but at the same time they labor day and night, working the land and readying it for new life. God brings the land to life through them. James's exhortation could be addressed to us: "You too must be patient. Make your hearts firm."

Each year on the Third Sunday of Advent, we turn our gaze to the figure of John the Baptist. In today's Gospel we hear Jesus explaining the role that John plays in God's plan of salvation. Rather than invoking the Isaian passage about the voice crying in the wilderness (Isa 40:3), he quotes Malachi, the prophet who called for repentance and reform. This prophet spoke of a messenger who would prepare the way of the LORD (Mal 3:1). Jesus declares that John is that precursor. He points to John's strength of character and wholehearted commitment to his calling. This was not a man swayed by ignoble standards. John was a man of integrity, now in prison paying the price of that integrity.

This may seem like a sobering thought for a Sunday on which we rejoice in the prospect of eschatological fulfillment. However, it is John who heralds its approach, and it is John who reminds us that it is not a cheap grace. We would do well to take to heart the urging of Isaiah: "Be strong, fear not!" If God accomplished miracles of restoration before, through other people, God can certainly accomplish miracles of restoration today—through us. As God worked through John, so God works through us. But, as the farmer labored over the land, so we too must actively respond to our respective callings.

Our world will be transformed by dedicated teachers, honest news media, equitable business managers, compassionate health-care providers, and vigilant public servants, to name but a few. Today we stand at a lookout point and rejoice over the restoration that God has planned. But we cannot linger here; we must return to our respective fields, there to allow God to transform the world through us.

Praying with Scripture

- How does God work through you to transform our world?

- Inspired by the psalm response, do something this week that will contribute to the healing of another.

- What price does commitment to values exact of you? Pray for the grace to pay it generously.

FOURTH SUNDAY OF ADVENT
Readings:
Isa 7:10–14; Ps 24:1–6;
Rom 1:1–7; Matt 1:18–24

WHAT'S IN A NAME?

The Advent hymn "O come, O come, Emmanuel" is a song of longing and profound faith. But who is Emmanuel? Today's Gospel tells us that "Emmanuel" means "with us is God," and it implies that the child born of Mary is this Emmanuel. But what of the child in the first reading? Surely Isaiah had some other child in mind. Might there be more than one Emmanuel?

Actually, Emmanuel is more a title than a personal name. Many ancient people believed that kings were either gods in

10

human form or direct descendants of the gods. Therefore, every king was regarded as "god-with-us." In the first reading, Isaiah encourages King Ahaz to trust in God and not in the military power of those who would be his allies. He assures him that a future "emmanuel" (most likely his own unborn son) will grow up in a land of peace. Ahaz is told to trust that God will grant such a future of peace. This promise became a standard for proclaiming a future king and a future time of peace. It also nourished the people's trust in God. Though they continued to be disappointed in their royal leaders, they never gave up hope that God would some day bring that promise to fulfillment. And God would do this, not because they could rely on the abilities of some future Davidic king, but because they could rely on God to keep promises.

In the Gospel, the angel tells Joseph that the time of fulfillment of the promise has come. Though in some way every king was an "emmanuel," the child to be born of Mary will be the long-awaited eschatological Emmanuel. In a way that no other king dare claim, this child will really be God-with-us. The angel also announces the child's name. It will be Jesus. There is a play on words here. The name *Jesus* is the Greek form of the Hebrew name, which means "YHWH is salvation." The angel then explains that the child will be so named because he will indeed "save his people."

In addition to his personal name and royal title, Jesus is referred to in other ways in the second reading. Paul first identifies him as a descendant of David, thus acknowledging his royal origin. He also calls him "Son of God," another title that was used for ancient kings. When Israel applied this last title to its own kings, it was emptied of any divine meaning. But when the early Christians applied it to Jesus, they intended it to refer to divine origin. Paul used another royal title, calling Jesus "Christ," the Greek equivalent for Messiah, "the anointed one of God." Finally, perhaps the most familiar title that Paul used is "Lord." While this is a common title of respect, when applied to Jesus it contains divine connotations, because *kýrios* (Lord) became the Greek substitute for YHWH, the personal name for God in the Hebrew tradition.

All the names found in today's readings are statements of faith. We may not realize their boldness, because we have become so familiar with them, particularly during this season of Advent. If we look more closely, however, we might discover the challenges they pose. First, do we really believe that God is with us, as real to us as a child is? One's entire life changes with the birth of a child. Relationships are altered; priorities are reordered; schedules are rearranged. Has anything like this happened in our lives as we claim to believe that God is with us? Ahaz was told that the "emmanuel" who would come into his life would be a reminder to trust in God rather than in human ability or accomplishment. Has our commitment to Emmanuel made a comparable change in our lives? Do we really trust in God, or do we still expect to accomplish by ourselves what we have set out to do?

And what do we make of the name *Jesus*? In years past, children were taught to bow their heads at mention of that name. Today, it is frequently used to punctuate exclamations. Do we use it as an acknowledgement of salvation? Do we even acknowledge our need for salvation? People who suffer from various forms of addiction tell us that they know they will only be "saved" if they commit their lives to some force beyond themselves. How desperate must we get before we realize that in many ways we all need to be saved from ourselves?

As Son of God, Jesus has the power to deliver us. Do we believe this? The readings for today point out the importance of trust in God. Through Isaiah, God told Ahaz to trust that the nation would be safe. At first Ahaz may have avoided the threat referred to in this reading, but eventually he did make an alliance that brought disaster to the nation. Through the angel, Joseph was told to trust that the child Mary was carrying was the savior of the world. Unlike Ahaz, Joseph placed his trust in this incomprehensible mystery, and we have all benefited from his decision.

What do these names mean to us?

Praying with Scripture

- How might the realization that "God is with us" change your life?

- Use the name *Jesus* as a mantra, realizing that you are calling on him to save you.

- From what in your life do you need to be saved?

Christmas Season

CHRISTMAS
Readings:
(Midnight) Isa 9:1–6; Ps 96:1–3, 11–13;
Titus 2:11–14; Luke 2:1–14; (Dawn) Isa 62:11–12;
Ps 97:1, 6, 11–12; Titus 3:4–7; Luke 2:15–20;
(Day) Isa 52:7–10; Ps 98:1–6;
Heb 1:1–6; John 1:1–18

Do You Hear What I Hear?

At Christmastime we hear wonderful sounds and voices that seem to be silent the rest of the year. We hear lighthearted jingling bells that delight us. We sing beloved carols that express messages simple enough for children to understand yet profound enough to challenge us for the rest of our lives. We exchange greetings of peace and joy and love. This is an unusual time of the year, even for the Scrooges among us. However, the real meaning of Christmas is the spirit that inspires all of these touching practices, these warming sounds. If we are attentive, we can hear the true meaning of Christmastime proclaimed anew in the readings for this remarkable day.

The spirit of Midnight Mass is captured in a phrase from Paul: "The grace of God has appeared, saving all...." Here we find the meaning of the feast itself. The phrase also provides a lens through which one might understand the other readings for Midnight Mass. Isaiah announces the birth of a Davidic king who will usher in a time of justice and peace: "For a child is born to us, a son is given to us." Herein lies the messianic hope associated with the Davidic family: "They will name him Wonder-Counselor, God-Hero, Father-Forever, Prince of Peace."

This was the heart of Isaiah's message of hope. However, today this message is no longer a future promise, for "the grace of God has appeared." In the Gospel the shepherds are told that the child who has been born has come as savior. For this reason we might cry out with the shepherds: "The grace of God has appeared." Now, if we really hear this message and take it to heart, perhaps the Christmas greetings that we extend to others will actually be promises that we will do what we can to bring about the meaning of these wishes in the lives of others.

The Mass at Dawn, traditionally called the Shepherds' Mass, contains a phrase from Isaiah that brings into focus the liturgical themes of that Mass: "They shall be called the holy people, the redeemed of the LORD." Many people today have romanticized the shepherds whom we have come to know at Christmastime. However, shepherds were often despised because, due to their frequent contact with birth and death blood, they were regarded as ritually unclean and unfit to participate in liturgical ceremonies. Despite this, or maybe because of it, the message of salvation was announced first to them, and they were the first ones to pay homage to the child. Though considered unclean by some, they were really "holy people, the redeemed of the LORD."

Paul reminds us that we too have been made holy people through our baptism. We are a people who have been cleansed by him and made his own. Now, if we really hear this message and take it to heart, we will be attentive to those who have been ignored and despised by others, not simply because we are generous, but because they are often God's agents of salvation in the world. These poor and neglected people may be agents of God's grace in our lives.

Finally, the themes of the Mass for Christmas Day converge in yet another passage from Isaiah: "How beautiful upon the mountains are the feet of him who brings glad tidings, announcing peace, bearing good news." And what was the good news that this ancient messenger brought? "They see directly, before their eyes, the LORD restoring Zion." And if God restored the ravaged Zion of old, surely God can restore Baghdad, and Darfur, and Kabul. In the picture painted by the prophet, the people who suffered unimaginable devastation are being comforted, and peace is being restored. No more hopeful scene can be imagined.

Now, if we really hear this message, we will realize that miracles can happen, and they can unfold before our very eyes because we are the ones through whom God can accomplish them. The author of the Letter to the Hebrews tells us that this new child is the very Son of God, with the power of God to accomplish all things. This child was born to begin the work of restoration and peace building, a work that we must now continue so that all the ends of the earth will see the saving power of God.

This is the profound reality to which the delicate Christmas bells call us. If we examine the lyrics of the Christmas carols, we will discover there this same challenge posed to us today. And finally, the wishes that we extend to those closest to us as well as to perfect strangers will be more like promises, promises of peace and joy and love that we fully intend to keep. Christmas is truly the feast of glad tidings, not only that a child is born, but that the whole world is reborn.

Praying with Scripture

- Take a moment to give thanks for the ways the grace of God has appeared in your life.

- As you wish others the joy of Christmas, think of new ways that you might bring this joy about in their lives

- Take steps to resolve some estrangement that exists in your own life.

HOLY FAMILY
Readings:
Sir 3:2–7, 12–14; Ps 128:1–5;
Col 3:12–21; Matt 2:13–15, 19–23

FAMILY TIES

Family-oriented sitcoms may produce a good laugh, but they do not always model healthy relationships. They often feature children who constantly outsmart their parents, or parents preoccupied with their own interests, neglecting their children. The media even grants awards to programs that highlight dysfunctional families. The readings for today's feast provide us with a very different point of view. The first reading concentrates on the responsibilities children have toward their parents; the second illustrates parents' care for their child.

Sirach, a book from the Wisdom tradition of ancient Israel, insists that children are to honor both father and mother. The admonition to care for an elderly parent shows that the instruction found in this passage was addressed to adult children, not merely to youth. However, if this duty to honor one's parents is not instilled in the early years, only with great difficulty will it develop later. Elders should be honored because they are the repositories of wisdom gleaned from life. Their hard work has earned the benefits enjoyed by the generations that follow them. They should never be pushed aside and disregarded. Rather, they deserve our respect, our gratitude, and whatever care they require.

Such an attitude of respect for elders may be almost countercultural for a society that seems to enshrine youth. When children or young people are made to think that the sun rises and sets on them, as often happens with sports or entertainment celebrities, they may feel bereft when they grow older and are put aside for yet younger people. And they are not the only ones adversely affected by such a misguided point of view. This kind of inappropriate adulation does not help people understand the proper place of the young in society or the respect due to elders.

In the Gospel, Mary and Joseph are warned of the danger facing the child. They put aside their own plans in order to secure his safety. One would think that such unselfishness is inherent in parenthood. However, such is not always the case. The news is too often filled with stories of parents who neglect, violate, or even kill their own helpless children. Though it is unimaginable to most of us, children are sometimes thought to be burdens and, therefore, disposable. The entire society should cherish its children. It is reason enough to do so because they are defenseless. But in addition to this, children are the hope of its future, just as elders are the treasury of its past.

Paul provides a list of values that come to life and are nurtured in the warmth of the family. It is there that children first experience compassion and kindness and then bestow it on others. It is there that gentleness and patience shape their tender spirits so that they will extend gentleness and patience to others. It is in the family that they learn to bear with one another and to forgive one another. The author of Sirach is quite clear about this. This feast reminds us that every family is called to be holy.

It has been said that the true character of a society can be judged by the way it treats its elders and its children. These two groups often include the most vulnerable of the society, people who lack status and the power that comes from it as well as independence and the self-determination that it brings. However, a society's treatment of these two groups also reveals how that society understands and appreciates its past and anticipates and cherishes its future.

Another kind of family is highlighted today, the family of God. The character of this family is clearly sketched in the reading from Paul. There he calls the Christians of Colossae "God's chosen ones, holy and beloved." He summons them, and us as well, to "put on love, that is, the bond of perfection. And let the peace of Christ control your hearts, the peace into which you were also called in one body." It is blood that binds us to the members of our natural family, and it is love, love given us by God, that binds us to the family that is God's people. We are born into God's family through baptism; we are nurtured there and guided as we grow to full stature.

Just as society does not always value its elders or cherish its children, so it does not always hold the same values as does the family of God. Such values include: "heartfelt compassion, kindness, humility, gentleness, and patience." It too often advocates self-centered promotion, vicious competition, and a relentless drive to control. When these two sets of goals collide, there is often misunderstanding, discrimination, and even rejection, as we see in the gospel story.

The feast of the Holy Family with its rich readings calls us to renew and strengthen the ties that bind, family ties of blood and community ties of baptism.

Praying with Scripture

- What might you do that could make life easier for someone who is elderly?

- Do something special for a child this week.

- Show the members of your family that they are important to you.

SOLEMNITY OF THE BLESSED VIRGIN MARY
Readings:
Num 6:22–27; Ps 67:2–3, 5–6, 8; Gal 4:4–7; Luke 2:16–21

TURNING IT OVER IN HER MIND

During Christmastime, we have been particularly attentive to the child who was born to fulfill the promises made by God long ago. Today we focus on Mary, the one from whose flesh that child was fashioned. In all of the Christmas stories, she is silent, explaining nothing when visitors come to see the marvels that have taken place. Most likely, she did not explain them because she did not understand them herself. Today we find that "Mary kept all these things, reflecting on them in her heart."

The Gospel tells us yet another important fact about Mary: She was an observant Jew. She and her husband, Joseph, followed the Jewish religious prescription requiring that "every male among you, when he is eight days old, shall be circumcised" (Gen 17:12). This mark on the flesh signified that the child had been officially offered to God. Furthermore, this child "was named Jesus, the name given him by the angel before he was conceived in the womb," showing that Mary followed the directives given to her by the angel.

Paul too kept all these things, reflecting on them in his heart. But he would not be silent. He proclaimed them aloud wherever he went and whenever he could. In the Letter to the Galatians, he was concerned to show that Jesus was indeed a man of flesh and blood, the flesh and blood of Mary. Lest anyone suggest that Jesus was some kind of a phantasm, Paul insisted that he was human, "born of a woman," and that he was a Jew, "born under the law." According to Paul, the very humanness that Jesus received from Mary prevented anyone from dismissing Jesus as one far beyond us. That same humanness, which he shares with us, won us the right to call God "Abba, Father!"

There are times when the divine qualities of Jesus overwhelm us as well. After all, as Mary was told, angels announced his birth, and as Paul discovered, God had sent Jesus, both mysteries beyond comprehension. At such times, like Mary and Paul, we too must reflect on all these things in the quiet of our hearts. At other times, however, we might have to remind ourselves of Jesus' humanness. We should not forget that he was once "an infant lying in the manger," and he did suffer unspeakably in order to "ransom those under the law." This too calls for our reflection.

Furthermore, the excitement that surrounds Christmas, the lights and the music, the cards and the presents, the feasting and the guests can all prevent us from appreciating the real meaning of the feast. At such times we must step back and reflect on it in our hearts. We must mull over the fact that Christmas commemorates the incarnation, the mystery that claims that the all-holy, almighty God has become a vulnerable human being like us.

The blessing of Aaron, found in the passage from Numbers, is appropriate for any time and any circumstance. However, it is particularly fitting for the first day of the year, the day set aside in a special way to pray for peace. So many of our families suffer from misunderstanding and deep-seated resentments; neighborhoods are torn apart by poverty and unemployment; and communities are ravaged with racial or ethnic hostility. The world itself seems always to be caught in the throes of some violent war. We are in desperate need of God's peace.

In the Bible, peace means more than the absence of war; it means fullness of life. This does not simply point to an abundance of good things, though that is included. Fullness of life means that one has whatever is necessary for life, no more, no less. It is clear that praying for such peace, as important as that might be, is far from enough. For there to be peace, there must be universal fullness of life; and for there to be fullness of life for all, there must be justice. Pope Paul VI reminded us of this when he said, "If you want peace, work for justice."

On this first day of a new year, a day when Mary is placed before us as a model of one who reflected on mysteries she could not understand, and Paul is set before us as one who proclaimed those mysteries, and the blessing of Aaron is given to us, we would do well to consider the challenge of peace in our world today. We might discover that, like Mary and Joseph, we are called to be open to those in the world who are on the low rungs of society. Or we might see ourselves like Aaron and his sons, who were set aside for privileged positions in society, yet who had the serious responsibility of bringing the blessing of God to others. However we see ourselves, we are, as Paul reminds us, all adopted children of God, made so by the child who once lay in the manger.

Praying with Scripture

- Set some time aside to ponder the mysteries of God in your life.

- How does your life show others that you believe that God has come among us?

- What do you do to further peace in your family? In your community? In the world?

SECOND SUNDAY AFTER CHRISTMAS
Readings:
Sir 24:1–2, 8–12; Ps 147: 12–15, 19–20; Eph 1:3–6, 15–18; John 1:1–18

WHERE DO YOU LIVE?

"Where do you live?" Whenever that question is posed, the one asking is usually inquiring about our place of residence. At least that is the answer that we normally give: I live in Chicago, or I live on the South Side. The readings for this Second Sunday after Christmas presume that we have asked that question, not of each other, but of God: "Where do you live?" Both the first reading from Sirach and the opening passage of the Gospel of John provide us with answers.

A mysterious figure moves through the pages of some books that belong to the Wisdom tradition of Israel. We see this figure first in Proverbs, then in the Wisdom of Solomon, and in Sirach. It is a woman who is identified as Wisdom. She invites those who are looking for wisdom:

> Come, eat of my food,
>   and drink the wine I have mixed!
> Forsake foolishness that you may live;
>   advance in the way of understanding.   (Prov 9:5–6)

Wisdom is that awe-inspiring force at the heart of creation itself that calls to us, that enchants us, that leads us deeper and deeper into the mysteries of life. This wisdom is:

> ...an aura of the might of God
> and a pure effusion of the glory of the Almighty...
> (Wis 7:25)

Is Wisdom a divine force? A companion of God? An attribute of God? Or is Wisdom a god in her own right? However we understand her, we know that Wisdom was with God, "in the assembly of the Most High," that she came from God: "the Creator...who formed me chose the spot for my tent," and that she dwells in our midst: "in the company of the holy ones do I linger."

When we turn to the gospel passage we find Jesus characterized as this mysterious Wisdom figure. We discover that Jesus "was in the beginning with God," that he too came from God ("He came to what was his own"), and that he dwells in our midst ("And the Word became flesh and made his dwelling among us").

The mystery of the incarnation is so inexplicable that one attempt to describe it is not enough, and so we use various metaphors. Like Wisdom long ago, Jesus has pitched his tent among us. He lives in our midst, inviting us to a banquet: "Come, eat of my food, and drink the wine I have mixed!" He is certainly "an aura of the might of God and a pure effusion of the glory of the Almighty." We must remind ourselves of these issues as we gaze on the unassuming, defenseless child in the Christmas crib.

Still, we cannot long look at the innocent child without detecting the shadow of what will ultimately engulf him. The gospel reading alerts us to this reality: "He came to what was his own, but his own people did not accept him." In other words, he pitched his tent among us, but many did not recognize him in their midst. He was the light that "shines in the darkness," but some preferred the darkness to that light. We are not expected to linger over this shadow, but to realize that it is there. Acknowledging its presence should help us to appreciate even more the mystery of the incarnation. Divine Wisdom came among us knowing what would eventually happen. God lives among us, and this should cause us to look anew at how we live.

If Wisdom has pitched her tent in our midst, as Sirach insists, then we are bound to live lives that manifest that wisdom. The gospel writer tells us that when we accept the Word who pitched his tent in our midst we will be given "power to become children of God"; we will participate in the fullness that is his. The helpless newborn child will accomplish all of this in our lives. How can this happen? We cannot emphasize enough the power of the incarnation. God lives in our midst, and because of this, all things are possible.

How would our lives be different if we were to follow the lead of Wisdom? First, we would have a better appreciation of the goodness of our fragile human nature. Though limited, it is truly a marvelous creation. It was good enough for God to embrace, and so we should highly revere it. If we truly cherish the human nature that we now share with Jesus, we will look with new eyes at those others with whom we share that same human nature, all those whom we might have considered "most unlikely" bearers of divine mystery. The incarnation should lead us, not only to praise God, but also to respect others. If we really believed that God lives in our midst, we would certainly prefer the light over the darkness. We would open ourselves to new insights, new people, and new possibilities. Though the Christmas story tells of rejection, it also calls us to openhearted acceptance of the God who comes to live with us.

Praying with Scripture

- In what ways have you recognized the presence of God in your life?

- To what new insights might Wisdom be calling you?

- Pray for the grace to be open to the light that has enlightened the world, regardless of the challenges that this might bring.

EPIPHANY
Readings:
Isa 60:1–6; Ps 72:1–2, 7–8, 10–13;
Eph 3:2–3a, 5–6; Matt 2:1–12

COME ONE, COME ALL!

The feast of the Epiphany brings our attention back to Jerusalem and to the newly born infant. In some parts of the world, this feast is celebrated as "Little Christmas," with the exchange of gifts occurring at this time. With the coming of the men from the East, the manger scene is complete and, in a sense, the purpose of the incarnation is fulfilled. The very first reading for the First Sunday of Advent included a promise: "All nations shall stream toward [the mountain of the LORD's house]" (Isa 2:2). Today we see this promise fulfilled. Magi from the East arrive to pay homage to the newborn king. The mystery of the incarnation has been manifested to the entire world.

The Gospel does not say much about these men, other than they came from the East bearing gifts. However, apocryphal stories grew up to enhance the sparse biblical data. It is there that we even find their names. According to the tradition of the Eastern Church, there were really twelve Magi. The Western tradition maintains that there were three, corresponding to the three gifts of gold, frankincense, and myrrh mentioned in the Gospel itself. In that tradition, these three visitors represented the three major races of the then-known world: Melchior represented the black-skinned people; Balthasar, the Asians; and Gaspar, the Europeans. Their racial diversity signified the universal character of God's saving grace.

The star, which many today believe was the result of the convergence of several astral phenomena, suggests that these men possessed significant astronomical knowledge, a characteristic of ancient sages. Over the years, the star came to signify enlightenment. The reading from Isaiah, which speaks of Jerusalem's rescue from darkness, reinforces this theme of enlightenment today. However, Jerusalem was not alone in being led into the light; Isaiah says that all nations will be so blessed. Paul echoes this theme when he states that "the Gentiles are coheirs, members of the same body." It is clear that both ancient Israel and early Christianity believed that God's loving-kindness was open to all peoples, regardless of race or ethnic origin. The revelation of God does not distinguish between social classes either. Today's psalm response speaks of the kings of Tarshish, the Isles, Arabia, and Seba as well as the poor and afflicted and lowly ones. All peoples rejoice in the glory of the LORD; the signs of God's presence are revealed to all peoples.

The epiphany or manifestation of God celebrated today is characterized by extraordinary brilliance. This is particularly evident in the reading from Isaiah: "…light has come…the glory of the LORD shines upon you…shining brilliance…radiant." We must remember, however, that these words were spoken to a nation that had just experienced the exile, one of the darkest moments of its history. Furthermore, this dazzling light does not come *from* the people, but *to* them from God. It is a harbinger of a new day for the dispossessed, a chance to fashion their lives anew. While the gospel reading depicts a scene of praise and splendor, its rejoicing unfolds within the broader context of darkness, for "when King Herod heard [the message of the Magi] he was greatly troubled, and all Jerusalem with him." We must never forget that all did not embrace this epiphany of God.

The message of today's feast is very important for us to consider now, when there is such racial, ethnic, religious, and class intolerance in so many parts of the world. Many of our cities are torn apart by poverty and bigotry; sometimes our local parish communities are as well. We may even experience this kind of tension and alienation in our families. Today's feast reminds us that God has come to us all; we have all been called out of the darkness of our own selfishness into the light of God's love and care. If God has called those who do not belong to our specific circles, how can we reject them? In the world in which we live today, a world in which diversity cannot be squelched or controlled by a small number of people, we cannot afford to act like Herod or the leaders of the people at the time of Jesus, jealous of their power, unwilling to open themselves to a new revelation of God. Rather, we must take Paul as our model. Fervent Jew though he was, he insisted that the Gentiles should not only be admitted into the company of believers, the body of Christ, but should be admitted to full membership as coheirs and copartners.

Isaiah told the Israelites that other nations would be enlightened through them. This announcement contains a message for us as well. We have not only been brought into the light, but we are also now charged to be the source of enlightenment for others. The Gospel does not state that the Magi proclaimed the good news that had been revealed to them. However, such a tradition did grow up within the early Christian community. Those enlightened by the revelation of God become the source of enlightenment for others.

Praying with Scripture

- How open are you to people of other racial, ethnic, religious, or social groups?

- In what ways might you share the faith that is yours?

- Most churches display reading material in the vestibule. Make a point to learn something new about your faith.

BAPTISM OF THE LORD
Readings:
Isa 42:1–4, 6–7; Ps 29:1–4, 9–10;
Acts 10:34–38; Matt 3:13–17

DOWN COMES THE TREE

Today is the official conclusion of the Christmas season. For many, it may be a rather sad time. Gone are the brilliant lights that added warmth and lightheartedness to our lives; gone are the pleasant aromas of holly and pine; gone are the greetings of love and peace and joy. It is time to go back to ordinary life. However, we don't go back the same as we were before. We now have new gifts to enjoy, new clothes to wear. We may have made New Year resolutions that call for change. While in some ways today may be an end, it is also a beginning.

On this celebration of the Baptism of Jesus, the gospel account describes extraordinary occurrences. The heavens open and the Spirit of God descends like a dove; a voice from heaven identifies Jesus as "Beloved Son." Most commentators agree that this episode inaugurated the public ministry of Jesus. John's baptism was a devotional ritual that symbolized repentance and a willingness to reform. He realized that Jesus had no need for this kind of baptism and initially he objected when Jesus came to him. Jesus insisted, however, that it was important "to fulfill all righteousness." John prepared the way (see Mal 3:1); he represented the preparation for the great messianic event. Jesus made this connection with John and these messianic expectations, and then, under the power of the Spirit, moved into his own ministry.

The words attributed to God in the gospel account call to mind the words of the prophet Isaiah found in the first reading. There we encounter a mysterious figure known as "the servant of the LORD," a person chosen by God and filled with God's spirit. He was attentive to those who were somehow broken in body or in spirit. To them he brought comfort and established justice so that they would be able to flourish. This individual came to represent the compassion of God. The gospel writer reached back into this Isaian passage in his description of the baptism of Jesus so that Jesus might be identified with this "servant of the LORD." These words would also have laid bare the character of Jesus' messianic ministry. He would bring justice, but he would accomplish this with gentleness rather than through the strength of arms. He would be particularly sensitive to the weak and vulnerable, and his example would be "a light for the nations" to follow.

The dove that hovered over the water is reminiscent of the dove sent out by Noah after the waters of the flood began to recede. These waters were not merely floodwaters; they represented the primeval waters of chaos. In the ancient myths, only the mighty creator god could control them. Traces of this myth can still be detected in the Noah account. When the dove returned with an olive leaf in its mouth, Noah knew that chaos had been subdued, the danger was over, and he and his family would soon be able to begin life on earth again. In its own way, this is a creation story. Though the dove in the gospel account symbolizes the Spirit of God, the similarity of meaning here is striking. Like Noah, Jesus came out of the water ready to begin a new phase of his life. Here too, the dove alerts us to a new phase in the history of the human race.

The trinitarian character of this feast is obvious in the words found in the Gospel. At the baptism of Jesus, the Spirit descended like a dove and the voice from heaven identified Jesus as "my beloved Son." This feast is an apt time for us to consider our own baptism, the time when we too were identified as beloved children of God. Baptism is the most precious gift we have received, and it is given without qualification. Even Gentiles like Cornelius, or you, or I have been welcomed into the community of the baptized, for "God shows no partiality." As we did with our Christmas gifts, we must now make use of the treasures of our baptism. We have been clothed in the Spirit. It is now time for us to put on these new clothes and live new lives in the Spirit.

Just as Jesus' baptism inaugurated his ministry, so our baptism calls us to ministry as well. There are many ways in which we can continue the ministry begun by Jesus. We too can comfort and protect the "bruised reed" and the "smoldering wick." We can establish justice in our homes, our communities, and our workplaces. We can be eyes for those who are blind, whether their blindness is physical, emotional, or spiritual. There are many ways that we can help people to live freely. Finally, we can act as beacons of light to those who struggle in the darkness of fear, or ignorance, or despair. If we live in this way, God's words can also apply to us: "This is my beloved son [my beloved daughter], with whom I am well pleased."

Praying with Scripture

- Read the passage from Isaiah thoughtfully. How might you continue the ministry described there?

- In your own words, recommit yourself to the promises made at your baptism.

- Following the example of Peter, do something this week that shows respect to a stranger.

Lent

FIRST SUNDAY OF LENT
Readings:
Gen 2:7–9; 3:1–7; Ps 51:3–6, 12–13, 17;
Rom 5:12–19; Matt 4:1–11

A MERCIFUL AND GRACIOUS GOD

The psalm response for the First Sunday of Lent sets the tone for the entire season. It is one of the most familiar biblical prayers for divine mercy:

Have mercy on me, O God, in your goodness;
In the greatness of your compassion wipe out my
offense.

In this simple verse we find two technical words associated with the covenant: goodness (*chesed*), and compassion (*rahámim*). The word for compassion appears in the Bible for the first time after the Israelites sinned with the golden calf. "The Lord, the Lord, a merciful and gracious God, slow to anger and rich in kindness and fidelity" (Exod 34:6). This is the prayer of a sinner who is in covenant with God and who appeals to that covenant while calling on God for mercy. It is with a similar realization of sinfulness and with these same sentiments of commitment that we enter the season of Lent.

If this psalm is the prayer of the sinner, then the first reading for today is the story of the sin. Like every biblical story of sin, it begins with an account of the graciousness of God. It is important that we recognize this order, lest we think that sin is simply the transgression of law rather than a breach in a loving relationship. The passage describes how God first created the man just as a potter forms a piece of art, and breathed into his nostrils the breath of life. The man then became a living being. But life itself was not enough. God provided this earth-creature with the nourishment and beauty of the natural world. And why did God so act? Because God is gracious.

Not satisfied to be a humble earth-creature, the man and his new female companion desire to "be like gods who know what is good and what is evil." This is the universal and perennial sin, to want to "be like gods." And who has not "fallen" into that same trap? Humankind seems prone to sin. We set ourselves up as a law unto ourselves; we seek to control others; we reject God and enthrone human ingenuity. "Have mercy on me, O God."

Lent is a time to acknowledge our sinfulness, but not to dwell on it. We must acknowledge it if we are to appreciate the extent of God's goodness. This is precisely what Paul teaches us today. The sinfulness of humankind cannot be denied, but as grievous as the sin may be, "how much more did the grace of God and the gracious gift of the one man Jesus Christ overflow for the many." Paul contrasts Adam and the evil of human sin with Christ and the grace that comes because of divine mercy. According to Paul, there is no comparison; grace far surpasses sin. "In the greatness of your compassion wipe out my offense."

The gospel reading shows us human nature at its finest. Jesus is tempted, yet he does not succumb. Many scholars believe that this account reflects more than simple temptation. Rather, it draws its meaning from past events in the history of ancient Israel and it focuses on the messianic ministry of Jesus. And what were the temptations that Jesus faced? He successfully resisted temptations similar to those to which the ancient Israelites fell victim: grumbling against God because of hunger in the wilderness; demand for a demonstration of divine power; worship of a false god. The ancient Israelites failed, but Jesus remained faithful. The gospel writer sought to show that finally someone was totally faithful to God.

Many commentators maintain that this narrative reveals the true character of Jesus' messiahship. It shows that Jesus sought to satisfy spiritual, not merely physical, hunger; he refrained from using divine power simply to attract followers; and he was submissive to God's will, not his own.

We enter Lent this year sobered by world events. The horrors and inhumanity of terrorism and war have embittered our spirits; the devastation of natural catastrophes has seared our hearts. We have been forced to face our own human failings and the vulnerability of humankind generally. Despite all of this, the graciousness of God is offered to us. The unselfishness of which we are all capable is seen in the willingness of so many to step forward and help others who suffer terror, loss, and confusion. This unselfishness is really the face of our gracious God, encouraging all of us to put differences aside, to repent of our offensive attitudes, and to work for a caring and harmonious world.

Jesus' resistance to temptation is placed before us today as an example for us to strengthen our own resistance to temptation. He would have us move beyond a superficial pursuit of the pleasures of this world to discover what satisfies our spiritual hungers. He shows us how to trust in God's tender providence rather than merely test God's almighty power. He challenges us to worship God rather than power, or possessions, or celebrity. What will be our response?

Praying with Scripture

- What human frailty is keeping you from living fully in God's love?

- What might you do concretely that will manifest to another the graciousness of God?

- Make the responsorial psalm your prayer for today.

SECOND SUNDAY OF LENT
Readings:
Gen 12:1–4a; Ps 33:4–5, 18–20, 22;
2 Tim 1:8b–10; Matt 17:1–9

A SEASON OF HOLINESS

Once again it is the responsorial psalm that sets the tone for the readings proclaimed this Sunday. The "kindness" referred to here is the covenant love that binds God to covenant partners. This loving-kindness is the basis of God's compassion and generosity. God cares for those in need, and so "our soul waits for the LORD, who is our help and our shield." Examples of this divine kindness appear in today's readings.

The first reading gives an account of the call of Abram. For no other reason than that God loved humankind, Abram was chosen to be the progenitor of a great nation. Not only will God bless Abram and his descendants, but also all other peoples of the world will be blessed through Abram. This story reveals the inexplicable graciousness of God.

In his Letter to Timothy, Paul heralds God's goodness. He declares that God "saved us and called us to a holy life, not according to our works, but according to [God's] own design." Again we see that the goodness that God extends is not a reward for righteous living. We have done nothing to deserve it. It is a free gift from God. Rather than compensation for righteous living, this good gift is the very impetus for conversion and change of life.

Paul takes a further step in his teaching when he insists that this grace was there for humankind even before time began. It is only "now made manifest through the appearance of our savior Christ Jesus." From the beginning God was caring for human beings, ready to pick them up when they fell, to care for them when they were in need, to offer them life in the face of death.

When we turn to the Gospel, we wonder: Just what happened on that mountain? The scene described is quite dramatic. Jesus seems to have been taken into another realm, a realm of light and brilliance. And he converses with men long dead. What does this mean? Moses and Elijah represent respectively the law and the prophets, the fundamental religious tradition of ancient Israel. Their association with Jesus confirms his authority and gives his teaching legitimation. The brilliance of Jesus' transfiguration signifies that this is a religious moment, a manifestation of God. It is no wonder that Peter wanted the moment to last.

The real moment of revelation was yet to take place, however. The apostles may have been transfixed by the change in Jesus, but it was the revelation from heaven that was more than they could bear. The voice from the cloud identifies Jesus as "my beloved Son, in whom I am well pleased." In reality it is God, rather than Moses or Elijah, who legitimates Jesus. God not only affirms Jesus' teaching ("listen to him"), but also identifies the intimate bond that joins them ("my beloved Son").

At first glance, nothing in the readings for today suggests Lent and the penance that we associate with that season. However, the readings do offer us glimpses of the kindness that God extends despite our unworthiness. Such glimpses make us want to repent of our sinfulness and change our lives. We may wish to stay on the mountain and enjoy the experience of God, as the apostles did. As Paul maintains, however, God has "called us to a holy life." Nor is it easy to leave our old life, as Abram did, and venture out into unknown terrain. But that is what we are asked to do.

As children we were taught that Lent meant that we should "give up" candy or movies, that we should "do penance," "say prayers," or "make the way of the cross." But Lent is more than a time for subtracting or adding. It calls us to look first at what God has done and continues to do for us. Out of love for us, God "called us to a holy life"; out of love for us, Jesus "destroyed death and brought life and immortality"; out of love for us, God gave us Jesus, the beloved Son, that we might "listen to him." Responding to God's loving-kindness will require some degree of transformation in all of us. Hence penance enters the picture. We may have to "give up" much more than candy or movies; we may have to travel a real "way of the cross." But we will accept these challenges in response to God's goodness, not as a sign of ours.

The gospel narrative ends with Jesus charging his apostles to tell no one of the experience until he has been raised from the dead. Between the transfiguration that occurred on the mountain and Jesus' ultimate transformation at the resurrection, he lived life in the real world. It was a life of struggle and frustration, not unlike ours. It was a life of fidelity in the face of challenge, a life that modeled the "holy life" to which we have been called. Lent is an opportunity to respond to that call.

Praying with Scripture

- Reflect on the many ways in which you have experienced God's graciousness.

- What might the "holy life" to which you have been called be asking of you?

- Make the responsorial psalm your prayer for today.

THIRD SUNDAY OF LENT
Readings:
Exod 17:3–7; Ps 95:1–2, 6–9;
Rom 5:1–2, 5–8; John 4:5–42

ARE YOU THIRSTY?

It has been said that we are children of the earth. The meaning of this phrase has been reinforced by the biblical story that tells how God formed the first man out of the clay of the earth (Gen 2:7). In reality, it might be more correct to say that we are children of the water. Life on Earth began in the water, and then developed out of it. Furthermore, the human body actually consists of about 60 percent water. We can live for several weeks without food, but can survive only three or four days without some form of water.

Many of us do not realize how important water is for a healthy, functioning body. We are told that we do not drink enough liquid, that we walk around dehydrated. We are also told that when we experience thirst we are already in the first stages of dehydration. Water is essential for life and health. It is no wonder that water is a very prominent metaphor in religious writing around the world. It certainly is important in the Bible, and we see this in today's readings.

The lack of faith of the people in the first reading is astounding. They have just experienced the miraculous parting of the waters of the sea, enabling them to escape from the Egyptian armies. Despite this, they have the audacity to question God's providential care of them: "Why did you have us leave Egypt? Was it just to have us die here of thirst?" Were their memories already so short? Did they doubt that the God who saved them from the deadly waters of the sea would be able to quench their thirst with refreshing water in the wilderness? What is God's response to such inconstancy? One might think that it would be punishment. No! God's response is graciousness. The people complain; and God gives them water.

The gospel reading tells us about a woman who goes to a well and there is promised water with properties far beyond her wildest imagining. Here too we see divine liberality. Just as the Israelites did not merit the water that God provided for them in the wilderness, so this woman is perhaps the last person to whom "living water" should be given. At least that is what we might think. After all, she is a woman and, in a male-preferred society, she is undeserving of any special privileges. Add to this the fact that she is a Samaritan, a member of the group that observant Jews considered fallen away from the true religion of Israel. Finally, she is a woman of questionable virtue even within her own society. Otherwise, why would she come alone to draw water from the well, rather than in the company of the other women?

As a man and as a Jew, Jesus would have known that conversation with this woman crossed the boundaries of propriety. But then, such boundaries never prevented Jesus from doing good. Besides, it is those who are thirsty who have need of water. The woman's words revealed that she was certainly thirsty. Though recognizing the impropriety of their communication, she asked for an explanation of his cryptic words. She came thirsty for water, she proved to be thirsty for insight, and she was promised "a spring of water welling up to eternal life."

This Sunday begins a special time in the instruction of those planning to be baptized at Easter time. The gospels for these "scrutiny" Sundays are taken from John rather than from the gospel of this specific liturgical cycle. Intended primarily for catechumens, they contain messages for the rest of us as well. Today, with the Israelites, we are told that God will quench our thirst, whether we realize that we are spiritually dehydrated or not. Today we see that Jesus is the source of "living water." Today Paul tells us "the love of God has been poured out into our hearts through the Holy Spirit who has been given to us."

There is no thought of our meriting these favors. The Israelites were undeserving, the Samaritan woman was undeserving, and we too are undeserving. Paul reminds us that "while we were still sinners Christ died for us." What matters is whether or not we know that we are thirsty; and if we are thirsty, whether or not we know where to find "living water." The psalm reminds us how necessary it is to be ever open to the goodness of God. "Oh, that today you would hear [God's] voice." We have enjoyed God's goodness in the past. We must trust that this goodness will continue. Therefore, we must be open to new challenges, to new opportunities to cross beyond restrictive boundaries.

These "scrutiny" Sundays are wonderful Lenten opportunities to look deeply into our own hearts. Have they hardened like the hearts of those who take God's goodness for granted? Do we test God, even though we have seen and experienced God's marvelous deeds in our lives? Or are we like the Samaritan woman, caught in the complexities of life, yet always open to new insights, to conversion of mind and heart, to opportunities for bringing others to Jesus? How thirsty are we?

Praying with Scripture

- How thirsty are you for the refreshing gifts that only God can provide?

- How open are you to new challenges? New opportunities to serve others?

- Make the responsorial psalm your prayer for today.

FOURTH SUNDAY OF LENT
Readings:
1 Sam 16:1b, 6–7, 10–13a;
Ps 23:1–6; Eph 5:8–14; John 9:1–41

Do We See Only What We Want to See?

Key concepts in today's Gospel reflect how many of us still face difficult issues. Like the disciples, some of us might believe that misfortune is indeed a punishment for sin. Like the blind man's parents, we too might be wary of standing in support of another if we fear that our own status may be in jeopardy. Like the man himself, we might be amazed at how God can work wonders in our lives.

Is misfortune really a punishment for sin? There certainly are times when we suffer the consequences of our own foolish or malicious behavior. But today's Gospel assures us that this is not always the case. In fact, the man born blind demonstrates not sinfulness at all, but religious openness and insight even before he gained physical sight. This man obeys Jesus' directions and washes in the Pool of Siloam. Furthermore, he responds with honest directness to the Pharisees when he is questioned about the miracle of his cure, even though he is then forced to endure their ridicule and rejection. Finally, his openness to believing in Jesus is without guile. This man's initial blindness is certainly not the consequence of any sin.

The parents of the man are faced with a serious dilemma: Should they support their son in the claims that he is making, or should they safeguard their own status before the religious authorities? They choose the latter option, and they abandon their son to the skepticism and scorn of the Pharisees.

Who in this story really suffers from blindness? The religious leaders refuse to see what is right before their eyes, namely, that a man who was blind now sees. The man's parents acknowledge the wonder of his healing, but lack both the religious insight to accept this marvel as coming from God and the courage to support their son in his moment of trial. Only the man who initially could not see possesses both sight and faith.

This reading should make us wonder: Why is it that we remain in our own blindness? Sometimes it is because of rigid insistence on protocol, as was the case with the Pharisees. In one sense, they are correct. Jesus did heal on the Sabbath and, according to the law, that is not acceptable practice. Despite this apparent infraction of the law, these men are blind because they refuse to acknowledge the divine power of God working outside the structures of their religious system. They refuse to accept the freedom of God and so are blind to the marvels that divine freedom can accomplish.

At other times we are blinded by fear. We are afraid that we might fall out of favor if we stand up for what we believe is right, and so we choose not to acknowledge it. We opt to live our own lives quietly and safely and not get involved in controversial matters. When we act in this way, we blind ourselves to the wonders that are unfolding before our very eyes.

The first reading highlights yet another kind of blindness, a blindness that comes from stereotyping others. We might think that these others are too young, or too old. They might not be the right gender, or race, or from the right ethnic background. They might lack power, or importance, or economic status. The prophet Samuel sought a king for Israel from among the sons of Jesse, but he considered only those of "lofty stature." He never even entertained the possibility of Jesse's youngest son, David. Yet this was the one whom God had singled out. So often we too are blind to the potential of others because they do not meet our expectations. We close our eyes to what they might become, or what they might accomplish.

Today Paul reminds us that in the past we all suffered some form of blindness; we all once lived in some degree of darkness. However, now that we have faith in Jesus, this no longer need be the case. And so Paul exhorts us: "Live as children of light, for light produces every kind of goodness and righteousness and truth." No longer be blinded by rigidity or fear or prejudice! Open your eyes to the light, and take brave steps into the future!

As we strive to open our eyes and live in the light, the sentiments of the responsorial psalm should encourage us. We may think that the miracle of conversion in this matter will be more than we can manage. However, we must never forget that the Lord is our shepherd, protecting us from all harm, giving us repose. With God as our guide, we can walk through darkness into the light and fear no evil. With the catechumens we are called on to make a choice. Will we choose light and all of the responsibilities that accompany it? Or will we remain in the darkness of our narrow-mindedness, our insulated lives, and our biases? As always, God is eager to restore us to sight. Are we ready to get up and wash in the waters so that we might see?

Praying with Scripture

- Does routine in your life and in your faith keep you from seeing the new reality that God is bringing forth?

- Be conscious this week of how you might offer support to someone in your family.

- During this time of Lent, pray for the courage to be open to truth and justice, even if you might have to pay a price.

FIFTH SUNDAY OF LENT
Readings:
Ezek 37:12–14; Ps 130:1–8;
Rom 8:8–11; John 11:1–45

I Believe; Help My Unbelief!

As we open our eyes each morning, we see life around us. We hear the whispers of nature, the hum of traffic, the lilt of a human voice. It does not take long for us to realize that death is here as well. It soon becomes very clear that life and death are both parts of the cycle of nature. Unlike the rest of the created world, however, we humans know that we will ultimately die, and so death becomes for us a specter lurking in the future, in a future that is a mystery for us.

In the readings for today, we are led past the inevitability of death to a consideration of life after death. Ezekiel's words are much more than a ghoulish scene from a Halloween poster. He is speaking to a people who have been defeated in war and deported to the land of their conquerors. As a nation, they are as good as dead. Through the prophet, God assures them that they will live again. They will be raised from death and filled with life. They will experience a new life, a life that springs from God's own spirit. Here we see that what at first appeared to be the triumph *of* death is shown to be a triumph *over* death.

The Gospel contains a story well known to us all. There we see three people whom Jesus loves dearly: Martha, with whom Jesus carries on a profound theological conversation; Mary, who believes that Jesus has power over the life of her brother; and Lazarus, whom Jesus calls back from the clutches of death. This account may describe the love among friends, but it is primarily a story about faith. Speaking to his disciples, Jesus says, "I am glad for you that I was not there, that you may believe." He then tells Martha, "Everyone who lives and believes in me will never die." At the end of the account we read, "Many...began to believe in him."

Just what is it that we are called to believe? Is it that a broken nation will be reconstituted? Is it that one who has died will be resuscitated? As wonderful as these risings may have been, they were not really lasting. At a later time in history, the nation of Israel would once again suffer defeat. And though Lazarus may have been given a second chance at life, eventually he would again face the inevitability of death. No, we are called to believe in something much more profound. We are called to believe in a resurrection that transforms, a resurrection that is lasting.

While the account of the raising of Lazarus is quite straightforward, Jesus' words to Martha are not. He says that either faith will keep us from dying, or, if we die, faith will allow us still to live. This sounds rather confusing, even contradictory. In both statements, however, Jesus is insisting that, while death certainly threatens life, it has no power where there is faith. This might help us to see that he is talking about two kinds of life and two kinds of death. Those who believe in Jesus, even if they undergo physical death, will still enjoy a bond with him. In other words, they will live some kind of life. Mortal life will end with physical death, but physical death has no power over the life of union with Jesus. Jesus, who claims to be "the resurrection and the life," asks us, as he asked Martha, "Do you believe this?"

Paul, who seems to have had some difficulty assuring the Romans of their own resurrection, understood what Jesus meant. He maintained that "if Christ is in you, although the body is dead because of sin, the spirit is alive because of righteousness." The basis of the teaching of both the gospel writer and Paul is union with Jesus through faith. Both contend that this union is not severed by death. Paul goes on to insist that if Christ was raised from the dead, then we, united to him through faith, will also be raised. The bond of faith is lasting, and to deny one resurrection (ours) is to deny the other (Christ's).

During Lent, we ponder these readings with their messages of new life. They assure us that our faith in Jesus, who is "the resurrection and the life," promises our participation in resurrection and new life. We are invited to join in prayer with the psalmist. We too stand before God and the rest of the world, guilty of transgressions. We have been selfish and deceitful. At times we are arrogant and lacking in compassion. We allow violence to devastate the lives of others. Despite these failings, we are invited to trust in God's forgiveness. God's loving-kindness can redeem us and lead us into resurrection and life.

Praying with Scripture

- Make the responsorial psalm your prayer today.

- Be especially compassionate toward someone who is mourning the death of a loved one.

- Pray for the grace to face your own death with Christian faith.

PALM SUNDAY OF THE LORD'S PASSION
Readings:
Isa 50:4–7; Ps 22:8–9, 17–20, 23–24;
Phil 2:6–11; Matt 26:14—27:66

HE WAS TRUE TO HIMSELF

The Gospel for today, which recounts the passion and death of Jesus, includes elements of intrigue, betrayal, and murder. A careful reading shows that the victim was not ignorant of the plots devised against him. Even before the horrendous onslaught began, Jesus announced, "My appointed time draws near." He told his disciples with whom he was at table at his last supper, "He who has dipped his hand into the dish with me is the one who will betray me." He foretold the cowardice of them all: "This night all of you will have your faith in me shaken." And to Peter's declaration of loyalty, he replied, "Amen, I say to you, this very night before the cock crows, you will deny me three times."

If Jesus knew what was ahead of him, why did he not take steps to avoid it? The reading from Paul offers an answer to this pressing question: "He humbled himself, becoming obedient to the point of death, even death on a cross." A phrase in the Gospel has Jesus himself affirm this sentiment: "Not as I will, but as you will." Such statements help us to see that Jesus was less a victim of fickle or sinful human beings than a willing participant in the designs of the very God he called Father. Is this in any way correct?

What was God's will, to which Jesus was obedient? Was it really his suffering and death? Or was his suffering and death the price that he was willing to pay in order to accomplish God's will? A subtle, but very important difference. In order to answer this, we might have to examine the reasons for the intrigue, betrayal, and murder.

Why was Judas willing to betray Jesus? Why were the chief priests eager to capture him? And why did the disciples desert him in his hour of need? The last question is probably the easiest to answer. When the disciples realized that open association with Jesus would place them in danger, they fled out of fear. This same fear prompted Peter's denial. Such fear is not uncommon. At some time in our own lives, we all know it. Many of us take great pains to protect ourselves. We are slow to jeopardize our personal security.

Judas's actions are not difficult to understand either. Some scholars contend that the name *Iscariot* suggests that Judas originally belonged to the dagger-wielding group of assassins know as Sicarii. They were a Zealot party intent on overthrowing the Roman occupiers. If this were true, then Jesus' messianic promise of a new society would have initially resonated with Judas's own political hopes. However, these hopes would have been dashed when Judas realized that this new society would be born of peaceful and nonpolitical means. If Judas thought that Jesus had betrayed him, he would not hesitate to betray Jesus.

Judas's disappointment in Jesus apparently fit well with the attitudes of the chief priests. They were the respected religious leaders of their day, the ones who interpreted the tradition for the people. They were the ones presumably able to discern God's will. This upstart from Galilee had no right to proclaim a message that challenged theirs, particularly if this message threatened the nation's relationship with Rome as well as their own. He would have to be stopped.

Thus Jesus faced the antagonism of the religious establishment that had compromised itself for political gain, the wrath of an idealist who felt betrayed, and the disloyalty of followers who feared for their lives. And all of this stemmed from the fact that he insisted on being true to what he believed was God's will in his regard. Throughout his ministry, Jesus presented himself as the Messiah of God, the one who would inaugurate the reign of God. His followers, including Judas, as well as the chief priests, were all longing for the appearance of this Messiah. But Jesus did not meet their expectations, and so they regarded him as a fraud. His claims were considered blasphemy and a threat to the peace of Rome. He had to be silenced.

Jesus accepted the destiny of Messiah as ordained for him by God. Furthermore, he fulfilled that destiny in a manner that shocked and disturbed many people. In a very real sense, Jesus was a victim of conscience, standing for truth regardless of the price it would exact of him.

Today we join Jesus as he proceeds to his destiny with all of the dignity that comes from integrity. Rather than concentrate on the horror of his physical agony, we might do well to examine ourselves from the perspectives of those responsible for the intrigue, betrayal, and murder. Are we willing to follow a messiah who may not fit our own expectations? One who exhorts self-emptying rather than self-fulfillment, obedience rather than willfulness, openness to new insights rather than stubborn adherence to outdated concepts? Are we willing to stand up for truth regardless of the price it might require of us? Are we really willing to take up our cross and follow him?

Praying with Scripture

- Spend some time this week reflecting on the passion account.

- In what ways are you called on to stand for truth?

- What price are you willing to pay for the sake of integrity?

Easter Season

EASTER SUNDAY
Readings:
Acts 10:34a, 37–43; Ps 118:1–2, 16–17, 22–23; Col 3:1–4, or 1 Cor 5:6b–8; John 20:1–9

WE SEE WITH EYES OF FAITH

Generation after generation, the Christian community keeps reexamining its teaching regarding the resurrection of Jesus. Carefully developed explanations continue to clarify the minutest details of this doctrine. Many of us are so familiar with these details that we may have ceased to be amazed at their claims: A man whose brutal execution was witnessed by crowds of people, who was buried in a sealed tomb, returned to visit his closest companions. Were the same claims made today, who would not be skeptical?

But these claims are being made today! In the Sequence we pray, "Christ my hope is arisen." Perhaps we too should be a bit skeptical; we should stand dumbfounded before its mystery. At least we should acknowledge that, like the disciples, we do not understand.

The honesty of the earliest Christians should never cease to amaze us. They are the ones who reported their experiences of the Risen Lord. They could very well have portrayed themselves in a better light, but they did not. (Today's Gospel suggests that the "beloved disciple" believed. But then, he was probably the religious hero of the Johannine community telling the story.) Most resurrection accounts acknowledge the misunderstanding that burdened the very earliest followers of Jesus. One would think that if anyone were prepared for this extraordinary event, those instructed by Jesus himself would be. However, Jesus' return from the dead was more than they could possibly anticipate, much less comprehend.

Accounts of the empty tomb do not prove that Jesus rose from the dead. They simply state that the tomb was empty. Even

Mary of Magdala, one of Jesus' closest companions, thought that "they have taken the Lord from the tomb, and we don't know where they put him." It took an explanation of the scriptures for Jesus' followers to understand what had happened.

In the first reading, Peter does just that. He begins with a summary of Jesus' public ministry as a way of insisting that this wondrous occurrence took place in actual history, and "we were witnesses of all that he did." As ordinary as its setting may have been, Jesus' resurrection burst the fetters of the ultimate historical reality, death itself, and there is really no way of understanding this. We often use the metaphor "life out of death" in our attempts to do so. However, that metaphor is an example of cyclical life, hence, inadequate since resurrection means complete transformation into something new.

If we don't really understand resurrection, how can we follow the injunction to preach it, or to testify to it? Paul answers that question: "Seek what is above" (Col 3:1); "Clear out the old yeast" (1 Cor 5:7). If we believe that Jesus has indeed been raised from the dead, then the way we live should demonstrate this. We will "seek what is above," rather than the greed and indifference toward others that seem to be so much a part of "what is on earth." We will resemble "the unleavened bread of sincerity and truth" rather than "the yeast of malice and wickedness."

Many of the Easter customs that originated in the distant past but remain with us today still serve as ways by which we demonstrate our faith in the resurrection. The new Easter outfit is more than a fashion statement; it announces that we have indeed "put on Christ." The tiny chick emerging from the Easter egg is more than a cute greeting card character; it represents Christ bursting from the tomb, eager to begin a new life. The same is true about the Easter bunny with its prodigious fecundity; it symbolizes the abundance of this new life. We may have preserved these Easter customs, but are they still signs of our faith and commitment, or are they simply part of the secular celebration of spring?

Will we ever really satisfactorily understand what resurrection means? Probably not, But then, how could we? As the basis of our faith as Christians, it requires just that: faith, not understanding. In his own declaration, Peter underscores the importance of believing. The gospel writer too maintains that the beloved disciple "saw and believed." The faith to which the biblical writers refer is more than mere intellectual assent. It calls for a living commitment that takes hold of our entire being. Faith in the resurrected Jesus transforms our minds and hearts so that we live lives modeled after his. Such faith reminds us that we have died, and our lives are now hidden with Christ in God.

We enter into the celebration of this great feast with faith, and it is this faith that cries out, "Alleluia!" All of the feast's symbols of new life are signs of hope for a world bogged down in despair and death. But they are not the only signs of hope. Our unselfish openness to others, our genuine efforts at peace, our willingness to forgive, all testify to the world that Jesus has been raised from the dead and that he continues to live in us. Proof of the resurrection is not found in an empty tomb. Rather, it is seen in the committed lives of those who believe.

Praying with Scripture

- How does your manner of living give witness to the Risen Lord?

- Pray that you might be open to the mysteries of Easter that you cannot fully understand.

- Recapture the religious meaning of one of your favorite Easter customs.

SECOND SUNDAY OF EASTER
Readings:
Acts 2:42–47; Ps 118:2–4, 13–15, 22–24;
1 Pet 1:3–9; John 20:19–31

IS SEEING REALLY BELIEVING?

The Easter season is replete with accounts of apparitions of the Risen Lord. The Gospel for today relates two of them. The first occurs on the evening of the resurrection itself; the second, a week later. The disciples' reported fear of the Jewish authorities suggests that they do not enjoy even a glimmer of the immense power of Jesus' resurrection. Only when they see his pierced hands and side do they believe. The absent Thomas is no different. He needs tangible proof as well. But if there is tangible proof, is this really faith? For we have been told that "faith is the realization of what is hoped for and evidence of things not seen" (Heb 1:1).

We should not be too quick to criticize the early disciples for their initial lack of faith. How could they possibly have anticipated the wonder before whom they now stood? True, Jesus had earlier told them that he would rise from the dead, but how could they have known that he was not speaking in metaphors? After all, the prophet Ezekiel employed the metaphor of dry bones when he promised the rebuilding of the disseminated nation of Israel (Ezek 37:1–14). No, the disciples could hardly have anticipated this wonder. And when it did happen, they could hardly comprehend it.

Frequently we occupy ourselves with trying to discover just *how* the resurrection happened. However, the basis of faith is belief in not *how* it happened, but *that* it happened. Nowhere in the gospels do we find the disciples wondering, "How did he do that?" Rather, they are overwhelmed with the realization that something momentous has occurred, and they are simply awed and stop in their tracks, without questioning. "The disciples rejoiced when they saw the Lord," and Thomas eventually professes his faith: "My Lord and my God!"

In today's Gospel, we see the reconciling power of God unfold before our eyes. The disciples are reconciled with the one they deserted out of fear for their own lives. Thomas is reconciled with the one he refused to believe had risen from the dead. Jesus welcomes all the disciples and commissions them to be agents of the reconciliation of others with God and with each other. This reconciliation is to be accomplished through the power of his resurrection. In a world torn apart by hatred and violence, reconciliation may well be our most prized Easter blessing.

The reading from 1 Peter was directed toward second-generation Christians, those who had never met the historical Jesus personally. Their knowledge of him came through the example and preaching of others: "Although you have not seen him you love him; even though you do not see him now yet [you] believe in him." This exhortation could be directed toward us today. Our faith too comes to us through the witness and words of others. Thomas initially refused to accept the testimony of his companions. When he did recognize his error, however, his proclamation of faith was especially profound. He did not merely declare that Jesus is Lord and Messiah of God. He cries out, "My Lord and my God!"

The reading from Acts is less an actual depiction of the early Christian community than a model of ideal communal living, the kind of living toward which we should all strive. Membership in this community was based on faith: "All who believed were together." Their faith expressed itself in various ways. The members were open to the teaching of the apostles. They both received and nurtured their faith on the word of others. Their faith strengthened the bonds that united them, and what resulted was an extraordinary degree of communal sharing. No one went without having one's basic needs met. Finally, the community came together for prayer and for the ritual breaking of bread.

The Gospel furnishes us with an example of one of the fruits of the resurrection, namely, reconciliation with God and with one another. The first reading cites some of the characteristics of genuine Christian living: openness to new religious insights, sharing with those in need, communal prayer and worship. The second reading alerts us to the price that may be exacted of us: "You may have to suffer through various trials." It is not that God wants us to suffer. Rather, faithful Christian living often comes into conflict with some of the standards and customs of the world within which we live. We suffer when that world rejects us or strikes out in anger against us.

The dynamic power of the resurrection of Jesus breaks through the doors behind which we have huddled, afraid of what the enemies of goodness might do to us. It invites us to foster openness to God's word, generosity in sharing with others, and genuine communal prayer. It charges us to be reconciled with others and to work for reconciliation and peace in our battered world. This is what it means to be resurrection people. Our Christian lives are the tangible proof that Jesus has indeed risen.

Praying with Scripture

- Take steps to be reconciled with one person in your life.

- What might you do to strengthen the bonds of community in your family? In your neighborhood? In your local parish?

- Pray for the strength and courage to live your Christian commitment even in the face of opposition.

THIRD SUNDAY OF EASTER
Readings:
Acts 2:14, 22–33; Ps 16:1–2, 5, 7–11;
1 Pet 1:17–21; Luke 24:13–35

I'LL KNOW IT WHEN I SEE IT

Many of us take great pride in our ability to recognize faces. Or it may happen that we are on a street or highway and we come upon a particular turn in the road or a distinctive landmark, and all of a sudden, we realize that we have been in this place before. At times like these, floods of memories return. What seemed unfamiliar is now familiar. Our memory works in such a way that we might say, "I'll know it when I see it." There are also occasions, however, when we do not recognize someone or something that we should. Perhaps our memory fails us, or the original impression was not strong enough for us to recall easily. Or it might be that people or places change so much for us that it is less a case of recognizing than it is one of being introduced to them anew. The readings for this Sunday are examples of the latter situation. The people just did not appear to know what or whom it was they were seeing.

We might wonder why so many of Jesus' contemporaries failed to recognize in him the Messiah whom they so ardently awaited. Surely Jesus' life and works set him apart from the rest. Surely his words seared their hearts, never to be forgotten. But that was not the case! Today's first reading tells us that only after he was emboldened by the Pentecost experience was Peter able to understand Jesus. Only then could he interpret earlier traditions so as to demonstrate their fulfillment in Jesus. With the insight that came from the Holy Spirit, Peter sketched the public ministry of Jesus through his arrest and crucifixion. He then testified to Jesus' resurrection and exaltation at the right hand of God. Speaking to his Jewish compatriots, he appealed to their common religious traditions to make his points. Peter "saw" this, only because God had opened his eyes. But would those to whom he spoke "see" it?

The Gospel recounts a second story about a lack of recognition. There we find disciples of Jesus, two people who presumably had known him during his public ministry, who believed that he was "a prophet mighty in deed and word." They now walked with him for seven miles while he interpreted the earlier traditions for them. How could they not understand it? How could they not "see" it? But they didn't. It was only when "he took bread, said the blessing, broke it, and gave it to them" that their eyes were opened and they recognized him. With that recognition, he vanished from their sight.

Both of these accounts show that people don't always know it when they see it, and it is not simply that their memory has failed them. In the first instance, the people did not recognize Jesus because he did not fit their preconceived expectations. Peter had to draw lines of correspondence between Jesus and earlier religious traditions. We should remember that initially Peter did not "see" it either. It was the Holy Spirit who opened his eyes. We are left to wonder whether those who heard Peter "saw" it. Did they have the faith needed to accept what they had not initially understood? On the road to Emmaus, it was the Risen Jesus himself who did the explaining: "Beginning with Moses and all the prophets, he interpreted for them what referred to him in all the Scriptures." And still they did not know who he was. It was only in the breaking of the bread that they finally "saw" it. In neither case were they able to understand without some kind of divine intervention. If even Peter and the disciples from Emmaus, all of whom had known Jesus, found it difficult to grasp the meaning of his life and death, how can we hope to do so?

Though we are so far away from the events of Jesus' life, we do have a religious tradition that explains it. These two accounts report the early Christians' initial lack of faith. But they also report their transformation. Once faith floods their minds and hearts, they are transformed into believing heralds of the good news of the resurrection. The formerly frightened Peter shouts his proclamation to the very people before whom he would have cowered earlier. The Emmaus disciples, who initially had returned to their former lives, immediately returned to the city they had just fled and announced the news of the resurrection to those who were hiding there. Initially, all they had were the early traditions. Today we have those same early traditions, but we also have their testimonies of faith. We should be better able to "see" it.

We still must ask ourselves: Do we know it when we see it? Have we heard the good news recorded in the scriptures? Are we open to understanding these scriptures in new ways? And what can be said about our participation in the Eucharist? Do we ever recognize the presence of the Risen Lord among us in our eucharistic breaking of the bread?

Praying with Scripture

- Develop the habit of regular Bible study.

- Spend some quiet time reflecting on the Emmaus account.

- Pray for the grace of recognizing him in the breaking of the bread.

FOURTH SUNDAY OF EASTER
Readings:
Acts 2:14a, 36–41; Ps 23:1–6;
1 Pet 2:20b–25; John 10:1–10

FOLLOW THE LEADER!

The Fourth Sunday of Easter has traditionally been known as Good Shepherd Sunday, since readings today elaborate this theme. Their particular focus today is on leadership. Whose leadership will we follow? In the ancient Near Eastern world, kings were often characterized as shepherds of their people, because they were responsible for every aspect of their welfare. This same characterization is used in the Bible to describe the providence of God (Ezek 34).

The people to whom Peter speaks in the first reading are cut to the heart when he accuses them of crucifying the one whom "God has made both Lord and Christ." They entreat him, "What are we to do?" In responding he exhorts them, "Repent and be baptized." He assures them that God has called them. It is now up to them to decide whether or not to heed that call, accept God as their leader, and allow God to guide them in right paths. In a certain sense, Peter is acting as a shepherd, leading his hearers in a particular direction and guiding them away from false teaching. However, he is actually pointing them in the direction of their real leader, Jesus. That is the one whom they should follow.

In the Gospel, Jesus employs the shepherd theme in two ways. He first contrasts the genuine shepherd, who is allowed through the gate of the common sheepfold, with the thief, who is prevented from entering through the gate and must climb over the wall in order to gain entry. Since herding was, and still is, a common occupation in that part of the world, Jesus' hearers would have been very familiar with the pictures he was drawing. Though several flocks were kept in this common sheepfold, the individual sheep recognized the voice of their own shepherd and followed that shepherd's lead. They did not follow the voice of a stranger. By means of this metaphoric story, Jesus is saying that those who belong to him will recognize his voice and will follow him.

The psalm response, taken from one of the best known and loved psalms, expands this aspect of the shepherd theme. In touching imagery, it describes the gentle guidance, the fierce protection, and the loving nurturing provided by the true shepherd. This shepherd is not simply a hired hand who does this grueling job merely for wages. Rather, this shepherd is the one who has forged a bond of care and affection for the sheep. The "kindness" referred to in the psalm is the loving-kindness associated with covenant commitment. It should be noted that this is the attitude the shepherd has toward the sheep, not the sheep toward the shepherd. God's love for us is boundless and incomprehensible.

The second part of the Gospel contains a slight twist to the theme of shepherd. Earlier it is the shepherd and the thief who go in and out of the sheepfold. Here it is the sheep that do so. Just as the gate is the only legitimate way in and out of the sheepfold, so there is only one legitimate gate. Jesus states that he is that sheep gate. It is only through him that we can enter the safety of the sheepfold; it is only through him that we can go out confidently in search of nurturing pasturage. He is our way to the peace portrayed in the psalm.

Today's second reading also assures us that we have been called to follow Christ. Here too the metaphors of sheep and shepherd describe the relationship we have with him, but they are used in a different metaphoric way. Earlier the focus of the shepherding was external behavior; here the focus is on inner disposition. Jesus is identified as the shepherd and guardian of our souls. The author of the letter is speaking to Christians who have strayed from the path of righteous living, but have now returned to their shepherd. The image is quite different from the standard image of shepherding, because sheep do not normally return; the shepherd must bring them back to the fold. In these readings, the responsibility of the followers of Jesus is emphasized more than Jesus' care for the sheep.

Following our shepherd may require that we follow him along the path of suffering. We are reminded in the second reading that he suffered for us, leaving us an example that we might follow in his footsteps. It was for our sake that he faced the dangers that often result from living life with integrity: "He himself bore our sins in his body upon the cross." He is our model as we too face the dangers of a life of integrity. But follow him we must, for that is the only way to righteousness. It is up to us to decide whether or not we will heed his voice.

Praying with Scripture

- Pray for the insight to recognize the direction that God is leading you.

- Recommit yourself to Jesus, the Good Shepherd.

- Make today's psalm your prayer, reflecting on God's incomprehensible love.

FIFTH SUNDAY OF EASTER
Readings:
Acts 6:1–7; Ps 33:1–2, 4–5, 18–19;
1 Pet 2:4–9; John 14:1–12

WELCOME, ONE AND ALL!

There is something very disconcerting about being accosted by someone who challenges you with the question, "Have you been saved?" This question is not as innocent or caring as it might at first seem, because it frequently means, "Are you committed to God in the same way I am?" In such instances, the question seems more an accusation than a sincere query. It implies that there is only one authentic manner of commitment, and all others are fraudulent.

In today's Gospel, Jesus assures us that there are many dwelling places in the heavenly mansion. In other words, there is room for everyone. Since each person is a unique creation of God, there will also be a uniqueness to each one's search for and encounter with God. This is meant not to enshrine every idiosyncrasy and regard it as akin to spirituality, but to acknowledge the diversity of valid spiritual searches.

The Gospel points out the confusion of the disciples. They are troubled that Jesus will leave them. He reassures them that he is merely going away to prepare a place where they will ultimately join him. Thomas's response shows that he knows neither where Jesus is going nor how the others will follow him. To this Jesus replies, "I am the way and the truth and the life." Philip misunderstands Jesus' claim that no one can come to his Father except through him, to which Jesus responds, "I am in the Father and the Father is in me."

The first disciples are not the only ones who fail to grasp the full meaning of Jesus' words; believers down through the centuries have struggled with them. The First Council of Nicaea (325 CE) had heated arguments over the nature of the union of Jesus with his Father. We profess our acceptance of its final statement on Jesus' divinity each time we proclaim the Nicene Creed in our own liturgical celebrations. That council carefully articulated the statement of faith, but who really understands fully this divine union? It is, after all, a mystery.

Jesus' words *way*, *truth*, and *life* call to mind the Wisdom tradition of ancient Israel. That tradition addressed the manner of living that will result in happiness. One chooses either the way of the wise (the way of truth), which leads to life, or the way of the wicked, which leads to death. Jesus states that he and his Father are one. From this it is easy to understand why Jesus would say that he is the way to the Father. Christians follow the teachings of Jesus, believing that this way of living will lead them to God and to happiness.

On the other hand, the claim that "[n]o one comes to the Father except through me" has also caused religious antagonism, sometimes even resulting in bloodshed. How are we to understand this statement in the face of contemporary interfaith dialogue? The Vatican II document *Nostra Aetate* provides the beginning of an answer to this question: "The Catholic Church rejects nothing of what is true and holy in these religions [Judaism, Islam, Buddhism, and so on]. It has a high regard for the manner of life and conduct, the precepts and doctrines which, although differing in many ways from its own teaching, nevertheless often reflect a ray of that truth which enlightens all men and women."

This is only the beginning of an answer, for we still struggle to reconcile acceptance and respect for other religious faiths with our own belief that Jesus is the way to the Father. The council document offers some direction in the midst of this struggle. "The church, therefore, urges its sons and daughters to enter with prudence and charity into discussion and collaboration with members of other religions. Let Christians, while witnessing to their own faith and way of life, acknowledge, preserve, and encourage the spiritual and moral truths found among non-Christians, together with their social life and culture."

We see in this document that the church summons us to discussion, collaboration, and witness of life as ways of dealing with the diversity among the religions of the world. Today's first reading offers an example of employing these means within the church itself. A conflict between Hellenist and Jewish Christians was resolved in a way that "was acceptable to the whole community." This conflict was ethnic in origin, not unlike many conflicts we face in the church today. Diversity is inevitable, and it sometimes results in disagreements. When this happens, the challenge is to address our differences honestly and to seek ways of resolving the disagreements with the kind of reverence exhorted by the church as seen in the Vatican document.

Jesus said that there are many dwelling places in the heavenly mansion. Since it is God's mansion and not ours, we have no right to presume that some will be admitted and others will not. This is in God's hands. All we can do is follow Jesus and continue in our struggle to understand the teachings he left us and their implications for our lives today.

Praying with Scripture

- How open are you to others' religious search?

- Pray for the grace to follow in the footsteps of Jesus, who is "the way, the truth, and the life."

- Make it a point to learn something about one of the other major religions of the world.

SIXTH SUNDAY OF EASTER
Readings:
*Acts 8:5–8, 14–17; Ps 66:1–7, 16, 20;
1 Pet 3:15–18; John 14:15–21*

LIFE IN THE SPIRIT

Some of the most poignant pictures flashed across the world in the wake of natural or military disasters are those of orphaned children. Their inherent vulnerability is compounded by their victimization; they seem to be wandering about aimlessly. With unguarded expressions they cry out with grief and fear. They are so helpless, and they look so hopeless. To be orphaned means to be alone.

It is not by accident that Jesus calls forth this image when announcing his departure from the midst of his disciples. They have been his close companions and so he knows both their strengths and their weaknesses. Their own vulnerability and dependence on him might well have compounded their need, causing them added anxiety. Without him, they could be overcome with grief and fear, rendering them helpless and hopeless. They could be cast back into their preresurrection state of confusion and disillusionment, to their state of mind when they thought that all hope had died on the cross with Jesus and they might have to face a similar fate themselves. However, Jesus promises them that this will not happen. They will not be left alone; he will send another Advocate, the Spirit of truth.

The biblical stories read during Eastertide describe how the disciples were progressively prepared for life without the physical presence of Jesus. A careful look at each Easter account shows that the disciples did not initially recognize the Risen Lord. Despite his preparation of them during his ministry in their midst, they were really not prepared for his suffering and death, and so did not in any way comprehend even the possibility, much less the reality, of his resurrection. By means of his many resurrection appearances, however, they gradually came to realize his presence among them. The readings for this Sunday and the upcoming feast of the Ascension reveal another dimension of his mysterious presence. Though he will no longer appear to them, assuring them of his presence, he will still be with them through his Spirit.

The trinitarian character of God is revealed in the gospel passage: Jesus asks the Father, and the Father sends the Spirit. Added to the marvel of this divine activity is the possibility of our own participation in the divine mystery: The Spirit "remains with you"; "I am in my Father and you are in me and I in you." There is certainly no reason for us to feel that we have been orphaned. Still, the realization of God's presence requires faith on our part. Jesus is no longer with us physically, nor are we granted resurrection appearances, as were the early disciples. His presence is no less real, however, and the effects of that presence are no less powerful.

In the first reading we see the effects of the power of the Spirit in the ministry of the disciples. Philip proclaims the Risen Lord to the people in Samaria. Since the time when the Judeans returned from exile and refused to allow the Samaritans to join in the rebuilding of the Temple, these two peoples were alienated from each other. Now Philip moves beyond that enmity, and the Samaritan people wholeheartedly respond to his preaching. When the church leaders in Jerusalem hear of the conversion of the Samaritans, they send Peter and John to pray that the Samaritans might receive the Holy Spirit. And it happens! The early church increases by leaps and bounds under the guidance and influence of the Holy Spirit. The church has not been left alone.

In the second reading, the early Christians are encouraged to live lives of gentleness and reverence, with clear consciences. They are told, "Always be ready to give an explanation to anyone who asks you for a reason for your hope." Their very lives are to be the sermon that is preached to others. They are also warned that suffering may be their reward for living such lives. Despite their suffering, if they are faithful Jesus will lead them to God. They will have him as support. In other words, they will not be alone. The exhortation found in this letter is meant for us as well. We too are encouraged to live in such a way that we ourselves become the evidence that Jesus has indeed been brought to life in the Spirit and now lives through us.

Life in the Spirit is a life rooted in hope. Most of us live lives that are quite ordinary. We do not experience profound religious manifestations. There is seldom concrete evidence of God acting in our lives—or is there? The author of the second reading would argue that there *is* concrete evidence. It can be seen in the gentleness and reverence with which Christians live their lives. It can be seen in their unselfish service of others. It can be seen in their search for and defense of truth. Genuine Christian living is evidence of the presence of Jesus through his Spirit.

Praying with Scripture

- Are you convinced of Jesus' continued presence in our midst?

- How does your life give witness to that presence?

- Pray that the Spirit will give you the insight and the courage needed to live the Christian life faithfully.

ASCENSION OF THE LORD
Readings:
Acts 1:1–11; Ps 47:2–3, 6–9; Eph 1:17–23; Matt 28:16–20

SEATED AT THE RIGHT HAND OF GOD

The meaning of the feast of the Ascension is found outside of human history; yet, its implications touch the lives of all believers. We might wonder just what really happened on that ascension day. Was Jesus actually lifted up? And if so, where did his body go? The space travel that this generation knows so well underscores the ambiguity of such questions. Astronauts have been "up there" and, while they have seen quite a bit, they have come across no resurrected body. So what does this feast mean? Both the first reading and the Gospel give a few descriptive details of the event, but it is the reading from Ephesians that tells us what Jesus' ascension signifies.

On the feast of the Ascension we turn our attention away from the earthly life of Jesus and stand in awe of the exaltation he enjoys at the right hand of God. Both his ascending and his placement at God's right hand are metaphors that attempt to capture some aspect of the mystery we celebrate today. God has exalted Jesus, this man who lived among us, who was put to death because of his integrity as the Messiah of God. Metaphorical language describes his exaltation, stating that Jesus enjoys the place of honor in God's presence. His being lifted up is another metaphorical way of speaking. It characterizes his transition from existence on earth (even resurrected existence) to existence with God.

The description of his ascension to God reflects a mythical understanding of cosmology. The ancients believed that after the great primeval battle between the forces of good and the forces of evil, in which the forces of good were triumphant, a palace was built for the conquering deity. It was from the heavenly throne in this palace that the victorious god ruled heaven and earth. This mythic scene may well explain the throne of God in heaven described in today's psalm response and in so many other places in Israel's theology. This also throws light on the meaning of today's feast that celebrates Jesus ascending to the place of honor at the right hand of God. The principalities, authorities, powers, and dominions referred to in the Letter to the Ephesians are probably celestial beings. Though we today do not subscribe to the same understanding of the cosmos, the underlying meaning of the passage is the same: Jesus has been raised above all other beings, even those that others considered minor heavenly beings. Because he has conquered death, everything else is also under his feet. Since people believed that part of the essence of a person was captured in that person's name, even the name of Jesus is above all other names.

These mythic ideas may explain the description of Jesus' ascension as provided in the biblical passages. However, they are mythic ideas, not historic facts. In other words, they do not tell us what really happened. Though the historical details are what might interest us most, they are probably the least important. As with all of the mysteries that surround Jesus, the religious meaning of his exaltation is so sublime that a mere factual description cannot capture its meaning, and so we revert to myth.

As mentioned above, while this is a feast celebrating the ascension of Jesus into heaven, the readings indicate that his exaltation carries implications for our lives here on earth. In the first reading, Jesus' followers are told not to stand looking up to heaven, preoccupied with what was in the past. Just before he ascended, they had asked Jesus about the reestablishment of the kingdom of Israel. He redirected their attention to the future, to the coming of the Spirit and to their ministerial responsibilities that will follow this coming: "You will be my witnesses in Jerusalem, throughout Judea and Samaria, and to the ends of the earth." As they stand astonished, looking up to heaven, they are once again redirected to the future. The two men who suddenly appear assure them that Jesus will return.

This new direction that is set for them is stated even more clearly in the Gospel where the Eleven are given a commission. With Jesus' departure, it is now their responsibility to continue the work that he began. They are told to make disciples of all the nations, to baptize and to teach. This is an awesome task! Will they be able to accomplish this without the physical presence of Jesus? Yes! Jesus promises that they will indeed be able to accomplish this for though he is leaving them, he will be with them always, "until the end of the age."

If we merely stand awestruck looking up to heaven, as did the early disciples, our gaze will be redirected as was theirs. The mission of Jesus is now in our hands. It is now our responsibility to make disciples of all nations, to bring the good news to the people of our age. The disciples were not alone in this task, and neither are we. Jesus' words are directed to us as well: "I am with you always, until the end of the age."

Praying with Scripture

- What of the past must you let go by in order to move into the future?

- In what ways do you respond to the commission to "make disciples of all nations"?

- Make the responsorial psalm your prayer today.

SEVENTH SUNDAY OF EASTER
Readings:
Acts 1:12–14; Ps 27:1, 4, 7–8;
1 Pet 4:13–16; John 17:1–11a

A TIME IN-BETWEEN

The time between the feast of the Ascension and that of Pentecost is a period of liminality, an in-between time. Jesus has left, but the Spirit has not yet come. God's promises have been fulfilled in Jesus, but liturgically we await the coming of the Spirit. We now live in the tension of the "already but not yet." Today's readings suggest that this liminal time is an occasion for prayerful preparation.

The first reading describes the intimate bond between Jesus and his closest followers. They were with him on the mount when he was taken up to heaven. They then gathered in the upper room, along with his mother and relatives, there to devote themselves to prayer in anticipation of the promised Spirit. They are now living in a liminal period. The nine days between his ascension and the Jewish feast of Pentecost comprise a kind of novena, a time for them to reflect on the wondrous events they have witnessed and to prepare for another wondrous event yet to take place.

The gospel reading is part of what has come to be known as Jesus' High Priestly Prayer. In the context of the Last Supper, it is a prayer of anticipation. As we read the passage today, we see that God did indeed hear and answer the prayer: Jesus was glorified. We have just celebrated the feast that commemorates his exaltation.

The union that exists among Jesus, his followers, and his Father is an important theme in the gospel reading, a theme found in last Sunday's Gospel as well. Today we are reminded that Jesus was sent by God to reveal God's name (a glimpse of God's very being) "to those whom you gave me out of this world." A distinction is made between those who accept what Jesus has come to give and those who do not. These latter are referred to as "the world." Jesus is leaving this world, but those who have received his word are not. They must remain in the world, and that is why Jesus prays for them.

In this passage, there is no mention of the Spirit who will be sent to strengthen the believers and to bring to fulfillment the work of Jesus. The focus here is on Jesus' departure and on his followers' continued presence in the world. However, the reference to glorification suggests some dimension of fulfillment. Jesus says to God, "I glorified you on earth by accomplishing the work you gave me to do." It is for this reason that he prays, "Now glorify me."

This glorification does not rest in Jesus or his Father alone. We see this in Jesus' further declaration: "I have been glorified in them." Having received Jesus' words, his followers have been granted knowledge of God, knowledge that is integral to eternal life. They now have the resources for remaining in the world and for remaining faithful in that world. Only one thing is lacking, namely, the Spirit whose spark will eventually ignite them.

The second reading assures us that this spark will indeed be given, "for the Spirit of glory and of God rests upon you." Here we see that the Spirit will strengthen believers who are made to suffer in the name of Christ. The antagonistic attitude of others is precisely what Jesus was referring to in the gospel passage by the phrase *the world*. One might say that the strengthening of the disciples by the Spirit is the fulfillment of Jesus' prayer.

Like the earliest followers of Jesus, and followers down through the ages, we too often face the disdain and enmity of "the world." This word is used in three different ways in the Gospel. Early in the gospel passage it refers to the created universe (John 17:5). Further in that same reading it means "human existence" (v.11a). However, the "world" for which Jesus does not pray is that realm of human life and reality that is resistant to God and the things of God (vv. 6, 9).

It is this dimension of "the world" that insults the followers of Jesus, that causes them to suffer, as is described in the second reading. It is the greed of some that results in the hunger of others, the selfishness that tyrannizes, the indifference that crushes. It is the pride in human accomplishment that leads some to claim that we no longer need God. This is the world in which Jesus has left his followers. If we are faithful to him in the midst of such suffering, however, "his glory is revealed," as the second reading assures us.

Finally, the responsorial psalm offers us an appropriate prayer for this liminal period. It is a prayer of profound trust in God. It opens with a plea for help, but follows immediately with expressions of confidence that God will indeed hear the cry for assistance or relief and will grant our request. Though Jesus has left the world, and has left us in it, we have not been abandoned. In a very short time, Jesus' glory will be revealed and we will rejoice exultantly. Until then, we live in an in-between time.

Praying with Scripture

- In what ways has Jesus been glorified in your life?

- How open are you to the word of God given to you through Jesus?

- Make the responsorial psalm your prayer today.

PENTECOST SUNDAY
Readings:
Acts 2:1–11; Ps 104:1, 24, 29–31, 34; 1 Cor 12:3b–7, 12–13; John 20:19–23

DON'T YOU WONDER WHAT REALLY HAPPENED?

So many stories in the Bible recount the wondrous working of God. In some of them, the events are reported in such unremarkable ways that one wonders whether or not anything exceptional really happened. An example of this might be God's revelation to the prophet Elijah in "a tiny whispering voice" (1 Kgs 19:12) or Jesus' changing of the bread and wine into his body and blood (Mark 14:22–24). Other stories are replete with astonishing natural phenomena like the thunder, lightning, and smoke that accompanied the revelation of God at Sinai (Exod 19:16–19), or Jesus' transfiguration on the mountain with Elijah and Moses (Luke 9:28–36). The Pentecost event belongs to this second group.

The first reading for this feast describes an extraordinary event. There is a great noise, like that produced by a hurricane. Then tongues of fire appear over the heads of the followers of Jesus. The noise and the fire are what were heard and seen, but what really happened? The reading says that "they were all filled with the Holy Spirit." But what does that mean? We are told that the disciples were then able to speak in such a way that those present from all over the world could understand them in their own native language. But does this answer satisfy our questioning?

71

The reading tells us what happened. The disciples announced the good news of salvation "as the Spirit enabled them to proclaim." We, children of the scientific age, are interested in the mechanics of the event: Did it really happen as described? Was there an actual noise? Genuine tongues of fire? And how could they speak in one language and be understood in another? None of these questions is as important as the one that is often omitted: What does it mean to be filled with the Holy Spirit?

Both the Gospel and the reading from Corinthians provide us with examples of this mysterious phenomenon. Put simply, it means that the followers of Jesus were given the power promised by Jesus to further the reign of God that he had inaugurated. The Gospel tells us that the disciples received the Spirit so that they would be able to exercise judgment within the community. "Forgiving and holding back forgiveness of sin" is a way of expressing complete jurisdiction. It is a way of suggesting totality, like flesh and blood, or east and west, or left and right. Having received the Holy Spirit, the disciples are given authority within the community.

The second reading, a passage from Paul, offers a more extensive portrait of what it meant to be filled with the Spirit. First, it was the power of the Spirit that enabled believers publicly to acknowledge their religious allegiance: "Jesus is Lord!" This was not only a religious profession; it was also a political proclamation. It meant: I choose Jesus, not the emperor. How many of us are able to stand up for religious values in the face of social or political opposition? The power of the Spirit enables believers to do so.

Paul goes on to speak of the gift (*chárisma*) that each one has been given as a manifestation of the Spirit. In this passage he does not explicitly identify these gifts, for his focus seems to be on the unity that is possible in such diversity. This is clear from his reference to the many parts making up one body. We have different gifts, different forms of service, and different workings or expressions of power. However, they are all manifestations of the same Spirit given to us for the benefit of the entire body.

So what happened on that first Pentecost, and what does it all mean for us today? The Spirit of God took hold of the first disciples with a force like a mighty wind, and they were set on fire with zeal for the reign of God. As baptized and confirmed Christians, we too have been seized by that same Spirit; we too have been given gifts meant for the service of others.

Pentecost is not simply the "birthday of the church." It is more than that. It is the feast that calls us out from behind the locked doors where, like the disciples in the gospel reading, we may be hiding for fear of others. It is the feast that reminds us that we are indeed people filled with the Spirit, people with gifts that the world needs so desperately: wisdom for a world searching for meaning, knowledge for a world seeking insight, healing for a world torn apart by violence, prophecy for a world in need of direction, discernment of spirits for a world confronted by competing forces.

The power of the Spirit worked wonders in and through the lives of the first disciples; the power of the Spirit has worked wonders in and through the lives of believers down through the ages. What wonders will the Spirit work in and through us today? Don't you wonder what will really happen?

Praying with Scripture

- What gifts have been given to you for the service of others?

- How often do you engage them for the benefit of others?

- Pray for the strength and courage needed to proclaim through your life that "Jesus is Lord!"

Ordinary Time

FIRST SUNDAY IN ORDINARY TIME: BAPTISM OF THE LORD

SECOND SUNDAY IN ORDINARY TIME
Readings:
Isa 49:3, 5–6; Ps 40:2, 4, 7–10;
1 Cor 1:1–3; John 1:29–34

FOLLOW THE LEADER

"Follow the leader" has many meanings for us. As a simple child's game, it is a case of "can you do what I can do?" Since leaders are seldom willing to relinquish their presumed leadership, this can eventually become a game of "you're not as good as I am." At other times, "follow the leader" is more serious than childish competition. We follow the leader in a parade, or there will be chaos; we follow the leader out of a burning building, or we might lose our lives. Furthermore, we follow political leaders by supporting their policies, and we follow religious leaders by upholding their decisions. In many ways "follow the leader" is really serious business.

We are now in a period of Ordinary Time that is really a kind of interlude between seasons. Christmas is behind us and in a few weeks we will be entering the season of Lent. This is a time in the liturgical year when, rather than focus on events that took place in the life of Jesus, we pay closer attention to what it means to be his disciples. On some Sundays, we will look carefully at the challenges that this discipleship presents us. On other weeks we will turn our gaze on Jesus, our leader.

The various titles ascribed to Jesus in today's readings tell us much about how he was perceived. John the Baptist called him the "Lamb of God" and the "Son of God." Paul referred to him as "Christ" and "Lord." Isaiah spoke of the "servant of the LORD," a designation the early Christians attributed to Jesus. Each title reveals something about Jesus, our leader, and encourages us to follow him.

"Lamb of God" is a cultic title. It calls to mind the animal sacrifices ancient Israel performed in an attempt to reestablish covenant ties that the people frequently severed by their unfaithfulness. Perhaps the most significant and best-known ritual was the Passover offering, in which a lamb was sacrificed in remembrance of God's deliverance of the people from Egyptian bondage. This meaning stands behind John's attribution of the title to Jesus. As the Lamb of God, Jesus makes reparation for the sins of all. If we follow him, we too will be led back to God. "Son of god" was an ancient title of the king. Initially it identified the king as somehow divine. Though Israel continued to use the title, it stripped it of any divine meaning. Israelite kings were simply human beings. When Christians attributed this title to Jesus, however, they intended to recapture its original meaning. They believed that Jesus enjoyed a unique and intimate union with God that was characterized as "divine Son with divine Father." This is the meaning intended here. If we follow Jesus, we too become children of God.

Christ is the Greek term for messiah or "anointed one," the long-awaited one who would inaugurate the reign of God and bring about its fulfillment. When Paul attributed this title to Jesus, he was testifying to his faith in Jesus as the Messiah. We too are called to follow Christ into the reign of God. The designation "Lord" has two distinct yet related meanings: It is the Greek substitute for YHWH, the personal name of ancient Israel's God; it is also the title used by the Romans for the reigning emperor. Therefore, when Christians attributed it to Jesus, they were making a very bold political statement. They were proclaiming that, rather than Caesar, "Jesus is Lord!" Therefore, to follow the Lord is to follow God rather than some human pretender.

As we saw in the readings for the feast of the Baptism of Jesus, when we attribute the prophet Isaiah's title "servant of the LORD" to Jesus, we gain insight into the character of his ministry. In Isaiah, the servant was called to execute justice with gentleness and sensitivity to the vulnerable. His ministry was not merely to "the tribes of Jacob," the survivors of Israel, but to all the nations, "to the ends of the earth." Jesus' ministry was also universal. Even John the Baptist proclaimed that Jesus "takes away the sins of the world."

We have been called to follow our leader, and through our baptism we have accepted this call. But what does this mean? What does it entail? First, if we follow our leader, we are reconciled with God; we enjoy the benefits of being children of God; and we embrace the reign of God. Furthermore, if we follow our leader we will work to establish justice, and we will do this with gentleness and sensitivity to the vulnerable. These vulnerable ones could be our children or our defenseless elderly members. They might be the fearful immigrants among us, or those who have been shattered in any way by war. Will we follow our leader?

Praying with Scripture

- Recommit yourself to Jesus by renewing your baptismal promises.

- What about Jesus most encourages you to follow him?

- What about Jesus do you find most difficult to follow? Pray for God's help in this matter.

THIRD SUNDAY IN ORDINARY TIME
Readings:
Isa 8:23—9:3; Ps 27:1, 4, 13–14; 1 Cor 1:10–13, 17; Matt 4:12–23

CAN YOU HEAR ME NOW?

A very clever cellular phone ad recently found a niche in the popular consciousness. Asked in varying situations, the question,

"Can you hear me now?" suggested that, with this particular communication system, reception was good anywhere in the world. That is, of course, if you were open to receive the call. This all sounds like a vocation ad—not merely a vocation to the priesthood or religious life, but a vocation to a life of Christian ministry. In other words, God calls to all of us: "Can you hear me now?" And because God's communication system cannot be deterred by obstacles such as buildings or by anything in the atmosphere, we will hear this call anywhere in the world, if we are open to it.

Taken together, today's readings demonstrate how the early Christians understood that Jesus fulfilled the expectations of ancient Israel. In the first reading, Isaiah proclaims that the people in Galilee, the lands of Zebulun and Naphtali, who were in the throes of political crisis and intrigue, are delivered by God from darkness and hardship. The Gospel refers to this passage when describing the ministry of Jesus. This was the gospel writer's way of showing that Jesus did in his day what God accomplished in earlier times, thus characterizing Jesus as one wielding divine power. The Gospel then goes on to describe the call of the first disciples. It claims that those who followed Jesus would soon perform the same wondrous works that he performed.

The gospel reading recounts Jesus' call to two sets of brothers: Peter and Andrew, James and John. They were all fishermen. With simple, direct, forceful words, he invites them: "Come after me." Their response is immediate and total. They leave their trade and follow him. More than that, James and John leave their father. In a patriarchal society, the father-son relationship is one of the most intimate bonds. It suggests family responsibilities and the family business, as well as the family inheritance. To leave their father was a serious act of severing kinship ties. These men are called *from* their previous lives of family and fishing *to* new lives of community and teaching and healing.

The response of these men to their call to discipleship may appear to be quite radical. Actually, very few of us are asked to leave all behind and launch out into totally new lives and new ministerial responsibilities. Most of us are expected to answer the call and remain where we are, doing what we do, but now doing it with a view to proclaiming explicitly with our lives the gospel of the reign of God. Women and men will continue to be loving parents, but they will form their children to be good citizens of the reign of God, not merely of a civic society. Shop owners and clerks will continue to transact business with fairness, but they will be inspired by values of integrity, not merely for economic benefits. Professional people will continue to protect the common good, but they will do so out of vigilance for others, not simply as an exercise of power. The call may not demand a radical departure from ordinary life, but it does require a radical way of being faithful in the ordinariness of that life.

In the second reading, Paul warns us of the danger of clinging to religious heroes rather than to Christ. It seems that the Christians in the Corinthian community were claiming religious superiority because of the particular version of the gospel they followed. Some boasted of being followers of Cephas (Peter); others claimed to belong to Paul or someone by the name of Apollos; still others maintained that they were members of the "Christ" party. This is evidence that they forgot that Christ called them all, though through the agency of different Christian disciples. Their call to discipleship did not make them humbly grateful for God's election of them, but inappropriately proud of their status as followers of the followers of Christ.

We are no different today, we who boast of adhering to the views of some prominent theologian or spiritual writer in opposition to the views advanced by other equally prominent persons. Some take pride in maintaining traditional ways of faith and practice, while others boast of being led by the Spirit into new ways of being faithful. Paul would challenge those of us who often take partisan sides on religious matters: "Is Christ divided?" Despite our differences, we must remember that it is Christ who calls us, and it is Christ to whom we all owe our allegiance. It is now up to each one of us to discover how we might continue to proclaim the gospel of the reign of God. If we are preoccupied with our differences, we may not be open to receive the call.

Praying with Scripture

- How does your life today proclaim the gospel message?

- In what ways might you be responsible for divisions within the community?

- In what ways might you be a source of healing in the life of another person near you?

FOURTH SUNDAY IN ORDINARY TIME
Readings:
Zeph 2:3; 3:12–13; Ps 146:6–10;
1 Cor 1:26–31; Matt 5:1–12a

WHO ARE THE MOVERS AND THE SHAKERS?

Idealistic youth are not the only people who yearn to change the world. Committed social workers and politicians share that desire, as do scientific and medical researchers. Parents always say that they want a better world for their children. Teachers too seek to equip students with the skills they need to make a difference. Who does not want to improve circumstances? The question is not: "Do we want to change the world?" It is, rather: "How can we change it?" And this is followed by an even more challenging question: "Who of us is going to step up and do it?"

Probably the first people we look to for this change are world leaders. They are the ones who make the major decisions in our world. They are the ones who establish our economic policies, who declare war, or who broker peace. They are the movers and the shakers. Or are they? Not according to Jesus. In the message he proclaimed on the mountain as found in today's gospel reading, Jesus maintained that it is the people who are poor, or sorrowful, or meek, or hungry for justice, or merciful, or clean of heart, or makers of peace who will change the world. They might have to endure persecution in the process, but Jesus insists that they are the real movers and shakers in the world today.

The first reading contains a similar message; it speaks of a remnant that will "seek justice, seek humility…a people humble and lowly." It is important to note that, according to the prophet

Zephaniah, the future of Israel was in the hands of a remnant. The reading is offered to us today to remind us that it only takes a remnant, a handful of people to begin anew, to bring to birth the reign of God. The psalm response reinforces this idea: "Blessed are the poor in spirit; the kingdom of heaven is theirs."

And what do these people do to change the world? Paul tells us that "God chose the foolish to shame the wise...the weak to shame the strong...the lowly and despised...to reduce to nothing those who are something." And who are these people? They may not be "wise by human standards," or "powerful," or "of noble birth." They live their lives according to the unselfish standards of the gospel, with love as their driving force, not according to the ego-centered standards of a selfish society with personal comfort or gain as their driving force. They are the humble of the earth; they are the ones who seek justice. Some of them are indeed world leaders and politicians. Others are shopkeepers, cab drivers, or firefighters; managers, artists, or newscasters; students or retired grandparents. They are people who do what they can to make life better for others.

The readings for today show us once again that God does not conform to the standards of the world, but, rather, turns those standards upside down. The Sermon on the Mount sketches a way of life that might be deemed foolish by many, but not by those who truly love. They will recognize the Beatitudes as examples of their own love in action, love that they already show toward their own loved ones. The challenge of these Beatitudes is the call to show this love to all whose paths we cross. As we live in this way, we do indeed change the world. We will be understanding in a world that disdains those who are different; we will be forgiving in a world bent on revenge. We will be unselfish despite society's admonition to get what we can by any means necessary; we will be patient in the face of society's demand for instant gratification.

But will this really change the world? Of course it will! It will change that part of society in which we live. And that is all we really have to do. However, if each one of us lives in this way, we will influence each other in our common task of changing the world. If we each live our lives in this way, "the way" that Jesus taught will influence those around us, who will then influence those around them, and so it will spread. Goodness can indeed make a difference. Jesus promises that it will. He assures those who will follow him that the kingdom of heaven will be theirs; they will be comforted; they will inherit the earth; they will be satisfied; they will be shown mercy; they will see God; they will be genuine children of God.

Finally, the fruit of such blessings will spill over into the broader society, and into the entire world. By following Jesus' admonitions, we can indeed change the world. It is then that we will all see that those whose lives manifest this remarkable reign of God are the authentic movers and shakers.

Praying with Scripture

- Who has been an influence for good in your life? In what ways?

- How have you been an influence for good in the lives of others?

- What else might you do to change the world, if only so slightly?

FIFTH SUNDAY IN ORDINARY TIME
Readings:
Isa 58:7–10; Ps 112:4–9;
1 Cor 2:1–5; Matt 5:13–16

THIS LITTLE LIGHT OF MINE...

Who has not heard or even sung the ditty, "This little light of mine, I'm gonna let it shine"? Children learn it and sing it with delight. As simple as the words may be and as airy as is the melody, the message is profound. In fact, it can be fully understood only by adults, for it is a proclamation of one's willingness to give witness to one's faith.

The season of Lent will soon be upon us. It is that time in the liturgical year when we reflect on our redemption and on our need for conversion. The readings for today lay out a plausible plan of action for transformation. They summon us to take a stand for God by taking a stand in support of others. Isaiah calls us to share our bread, a work of mercy that is perhaps more beneficial than is mere fasting. We are told to shelter the oppressed and the homeless and to clothe the naked. These acts ultimately came to be referred to as the corporal works of mercy: Feed the hungry; give drink to the thirsty; clothe the naked; shelter the homeless; visit the imprisoned; care for the sick; bury the dead. Isaiah also charges us to "remove from your midst oppression, false accusation and malicious speech." We can surely take this admonition seriously. According to the prophet, if we do these things, our "light will break forth like the dawn."

We may think that we have all we can do to care for ourselves and for those for whom we are already responsible. We may feel that caring for others is more than we can manage right now. We must remember, however, that Isaiah was speaking to a people who themselves had only recently returned from exile. They had to reconstruct their social and political world. They had a Temple to rebuild and religious structures to put in place. It was to such a community that Isaiah delivered his challenge. In fact, he insisted that their care of others was the condition of their own restoration. By implication, this admonition calls us to care for the needy in their need and not merely when we are secure and it is not inconvenient for us to do so.

The gospel reading does not list the works of mercy, but it does tell the people of Matthew's community—and us as well—that with the power of God we can transform the world. Like salt, our care of others will bring out the best in a world that has turned vapid; like the radiance of a lamp, we can enlighten a world that is floundering in darkness. We can be a city set on a mountain for all to see, a refuge and safe haven in a world threatened by hatred and terror. Once again, we may wonder how we, who are not important people, can accomplish this. The lyrics of the song remind us that ours is a "little light." But in darkness, even a little light is illuminating; even a little salt gives flavor; even a small city provides refuge.

The words of Isaiah and of Jesus are very challenging. Some might even be inclined to quake at their challenge. However, Paul's words today should encourage us. He approached his ministry "in weakness and fear and much trembling." He did not claim to have the eloquence or insight of the great Greek orators of the day. He had no intention of impressing his audience with his own abilities. Instead, Paul was convinced that it was the power of God that was at work in him. He could very well have made the lyrics of the song his own. In fact, the power upon which he relied was "power in weakness." It was the power of Jesus crucified. This is both the mystery and the scandal of Christian faith: The world has been saved by what appears to be human failure.

Again and again we read in the pages of the scriptures about God working though what the world might consider "weakness." Extraordinary feats are accomplished through ordinary people. Jesus grew up as the son of a carpenter; some of the apostles were fishermen; Paul was a tentmaker; we are store clerks and teachers, bus drivers and doctors, bank tellers and engineers. Like Paul, we too come to ministry in weakness and fear and much trembling. However, it is the Spirit and the power of God that work the wonders, not merely our own abilities. It is the power of God that allows our light to "break forth like the dawn," that makes us "the light of the world," a "city set on a mountain." Ours may be a little light, but if each of us lets it shine, we can indeed make a difference.

Praying with Scripture

- Choose one of the corporal works of mercy to practice this week.

- When you fast, also give some food to the hungry.

- Pray every day that we may find ways to break down the barriers that separate people.

SIXTH SUNDAY IN ORDINARY TIME

Readings:
Sir 15:15–20; Ps 119:1–2, 4–5, 17–18, 33–34;
1 Cor 2:6–10; Matt 5:17–37

THE WAY OF WISDOM IS OBEDIENCE TO THE LAW!

Few of us like to follow laws. They are often so restrictive. They suggest that someone else knows better than we do—and who likes to admit that? It is with such attitudes that many people erroneously pit the message of the New Testament against that of the Old Testament, claiming that the former is a religion of love, while the latter is a religion of law. But is the primary intent of law to restrict? Isn't it possible that at times others do in fact know better than we do? And to claim that Jesus himself pitted the religious tradition of his birth against his own teaching is to misunderstand Jesus' message.

The Wisdom tradition of Israel, from which today's first reading is taken, insists that laws do not so much come down to us from above as grow out of our experience of life. For example, we do not need some form of divine revelation to tell us, "Thou shalt not kill," or "Thou shalt not steal," or "Thou shalt not covet." Our need to feel safe in society teaches us that certain behavior threatens the stability of that society. These laws are not so much restrictive as they are protective. They are meant to provide us with safe boundaries within which to live. And the one who has learned to live within these social boundaries is not merely obedient; that person is wise. Sirach tells us that faithful living is a matter of making the right choices between "life and death...good and evil." Experience teaches us how to make the right decisions.

The psalm response is both an instruction of wisdom and a prayer. It assures us that God will bless faithful living. However, the psalmist does not advance a Pollyanna understanding of reality. Life is not a simple quid pro quo arrangement; you do this and God will automatically do that. It is clear that we are not always sure what it means to live blamelessly; it is not always clear which choice is the right one. And so the psalmist prays, "Instruct me, O LORD...give me discernment." This is another way of praying for wisdom.

Paul too speaks of wisdom. In the second reading he makes a clear distinction between the wisdom of the mature and the wisdom of this age. Once again we come face-to-face with the difference between the standards of the reign of God and some of those of contemporary society. He insists that the plan ordained by God at the beginning of time, though hidden through the ages, has been "revealed to us through the Spirit." This is the true wisdom. But once again, since it is not "the wisdom of this age," how are we to recognize it? Here is where the law steps in. The law is a guide to wisdom. To say it another way: The way of wisdom is obedience to the law.

Turning to the Gospel we find Jesus declaring, "Do not think that I have come to abolish the law or the prophets? I have not come to abolish but to fulfill." He insists that the law must be observed, even to "the smallest letter or the smallest part of a letter." But he also tells us that it is not enough simply to observe the letter of the law. Instead, he leads us to the very heart of that law, to the spirit that enlivens it. It is not enough to refrain from killing another; we must purge our hearts of the anger that so often flares out into murder. It is not enough that we steer clear of adultery; we must guard our minds and heart from the lust that can result in such unfaithfulness. It is not enough that we conform to the practices of society; we must guarantee that the systems promoting those practices do not privilege some at the expense of others.

In many ways the directives that Jesus sets before us are much more rigorous than the laws found in the Old Testament. Furthermore, if we examine his teaching carefully, we will discover that the motivation for obedience to these directives is not legalist conformity as some might claim, but genuine respect for the other person. In a very real sense, Jesus neither abolished the law nor added anything to it. Rather, he reminded us that such respect was the motivation for the laws in the first place. Without such respect, we will never really feel safe in society. It is actually relatively easy to obey rules. However, it is very challenging to discern the values that undergird the rules and to be faithful to those values. It is by pointing to these values that Jesus fulfilled the law. It is in discerning these values and living in accord with them that we will be both wise and obedient.

Praying with Scripture

- Which standard of today's society most challenges your values?

- Pray for the wisdom you need to discern what to do in such circumstances.

- Make the responsorial psalm your prayer for today.

SEVENTH SUNDAY IN ORDINARY TIME
Readings:
Lev 19:1–2, 17–18; Ps 103:1–4, 8, 10, 12–13; 1 Cor 3:16–23; Matt 5:38–48

BE PERFECT AS GOD IS PERFECT!

Be perfect as God is perfect! Now that is a tall order. Though at times it may seem that some people expect us to treat them as if they were gods, who would presume to claim that they are perfect as God is perfect? Yet both the first reading and the gospel passage for today instruct us to be holy or perfect as God is. Just what might this mean? We are really not at a loss for understanding this, because both readings explain what the admonition entails.

In the passage from Leviticus the people are told, "Be holy, for I, the LORD, your God, am holy." It then does sketch a plan for human holiness: "You shall not bear hatred for your brother or your sister in your heart...take no revenge and cherish no grudge against any of your people." The reading ends with a well-known injunction: "You shall love your neighbor as yourself. I am the LORD." This passage calls Israel to be holy and then immediately directs them to love others. The reason given for this love is the fact that the holy God is the LORD, the God with whom Israel was in covenant. All this suggests that to be in covenant with God requires that we live loving lives.

The psalm response is filled with covenant language. There we read that God is merciful and gracious, abounding in kindness, filled with compassion. Being in covenant with God calls us to be like God—merciful and gracious, abounding in kindness, filled with compassion. If we are true to this covenant commitment and allow it to transform us, we will indeed be holy or perfect like God is.

The gospel reading reinforces these sentiments. There Jesus declares that living according to strict retributive justice is not adequate for those who would be his followers. "An eye for an eye and a tooth for a tooth" may have been an advance beyond the kind of vengeance that was exercised in the ancient world and is often exercised today as well, but life in the reign of God calls for a different kind of interaction with others. The three examples that Jesus offers are drawn from social customs of his day. Rather than retaliate when insulted, his followers should respond in a nonviolent manner; they should generously relinquish possessions; and they should be willing to inconvenience themselves for others. In each instance, they are told to disarm those who offend them by their willingness to overturn "an eye for an eye and a tooth for a tooth" and to go far beyond what was formally required of them.

Jesus even turns the injunction, "You shall love your neighbor and hate your enemy," upside down when he insists that his followers must love not only their neighbors, their families, and their friends, but they must love their enemies as well. This meant that the Jews were to look at their Roman occupiers in a new way; the followers of Jesus were to pray for those who might persecute them for their beliefs.

The radical nature of this injunction becomes clear when we look at the circumstances of our own lives. What does it mean for us as a nation or as individuals to love our enemies? To pray for those who do us harm? It certainly cannot mean that we should overlook any evil that might victimize us. But it does call us to remember that we are all God's children, good and bad, just and unjust. We may not be able to shower blessings on the people as God does, but we must as least refrain from seeking revenge.

This directive to love is anything but romantic. It may be the most difficult directive required of discipleship. But we have been called to be holy or perfect as God is, and this requires the mercy, graciousness, kindness, and compassion of God. It requires that we "take no revenge and cherish no grudge." The society in which we live, a society that tells us that we should "do unto others before they can do unto us," would call such love "foolishness." In the second reading Paul responds with a reverse charge: "...the wisdom of this world is foolishness in the eyes of God." Paul claims that we can indeed live such unselfish love, for we have at our disposal the power of the Spirit of God. After all, "[we] are the temple of God, and the Spirit of God dwells in [us]." This reading ends on one of the most comforting notes of the entire New Testament. Paul assures us that what may appear to be impossible (being holy or perfect like God) is within our reach, because "everything belongs to you...and you to Christ, and Christ to God."

Praying with Scripture

- Pray today's psalm response, reflecting on God's gracious love for you.

- Recall how someone's unselfish love enriched your life.

- Ask for the grace to forgive someone who has offended you.

EIGHTH SUNDAY IN ORDINARY TIME
Readings:
*Isa 49:14–15; Ps 62:2–3, 6–9;
1 Cor 4:1–5; Matt 6:24–34*

IN GOD WE TRUST

The money of the United States, coins and bills alike, bears the admirable statement, "In God we trust." How strange that what is perhaps the most influential economic power in today's world features this statement of faith on its money. Trust typically flows from the realization of vulnerability and need, and these are not characteristics usually attributed to the United States. Undoubtedly the saying was more than a pious maxim when it was chosen. In its beginnings, however, this country, which was settled by many immigrant groups who came in search of religious liberty, was indeed quite vulnerable and in need. The saying probably reminded them of their dependence on God and encouraged them as they faced the hardships of settling in a new and unfamiliar country.

Today's readings all address some aspect of trust in God. The passage from the prophet Isaiah is only two verses long, but it sketches a heartwarming picture of God. As a result of their defeat by the Babylonians and their consequent exile in that foreign land, the people felt abandoned by God. We must remember that they eventually admitted that they brought their misfortune upon themselves by their infidelities. Therefore, if they had been abandoned, they realized that it was the result of divine justice, not divine capriciousness. However, the message of the prophet moves beyond the people's sinfulness and focuses on God's magnanimous love. God had no more forgotten the people than a mother could forget the child that for nine months had safely rested just below her heart. And even if by some chance a mother could forget that child, God would never forget Israel. Now this is the God in whom we can put our trust!

The psalm response employs several metaphors to characterize God. God is a rock, a stronghold, a refuge, a place of salvation—descriptions that demonstrate God's power to save.
Furthermore, the psalmist claims that God alone is the source of
peace: "Only in God is my soul at rest." The Hebrew word for
"soul" really refers to the living and life-giving dimension of the
entire person. In other words, it implies that there is calm in the
deepest part of the psalmist's being, a trusting calm that will not
be disrupted. Now this is the God in whom we can put our trust!

In the gospel reading, Jesus speaks first about loyalty and
then about trust. These dispositions are linked together, for we
offer our loyalty to persons, groups, or institutions that we consider trustworthy. Here Jesus refers not only to trust and loyalty
but also to service. Our dedication cannot be divided; we are
either committed to mammon (the things of the world) or to God.
Jesus is well aware of our need of the things of this world—food
and drink, shelter and clothing, occupation and amusement. It is
because of this need that at times they become the major concern
of our lives. It is not our legitimate need but a distorted view of
these needs that Jesus condemns. He assures his hearers that God
is like the mother in the Isaian passage. He assures them, "Your
heavenly Father knows that you need them all." Then pointing to
the natural world, he calls their attention to the fact that God
cares for all living things even without their asking for help. Now
this is the God in whom we can put our trust!

We are instructed to trust in God and not in mammon. But
what does this mean? If our trust is to be a truly religious sentiment it must be for more than a victory on Monday-night football,
or success in the stock market. The first reading tells us where to
place our trust and what we should hope for: "Seek first the kingdom of God and his righteousness, and all these things will be
given you besides." If we seek the things of God, we must trust
that God will care for us even though we may not know how this
will unfold. There is no guarantee that trust in God will preserve
us from hardship. We do not place our trust in *what* God can do,
but in the *God* who can do all things.

The drawback in being a strong, independent, prosperous
nation is that we are seldom called on to trust anything or anyone but ourselves. We should not have to lose everything to real-

ize that it is from God that we receive everything. It would do us well to remember the circumstances of our origins as a nation and our own individual, innate vulnerability. Perhaps we would then realize how God has cared for us with the tenderness of a mother and the care of a father. Now this is the God in whom we can put our trust!

Praying with Scripture

- Which people in your life do you trust? Why?

- Which areas of your life do you normally entrust to God? Why?

- Pray today's responsorial psalm slowly and thoughtfully.

NINTH SUNDAY IN ORDINARY TIME
Readings:
Deut 11:18, 26–28, 32; Ps 31:2–4, 17, 25;
Rom 3:21–25, 28; Matt 7:21–27

THE CHOICE IS YOURS

One of the signs of having grown up is the ability to choose for ourselves. It began when we were allowed to decide when we would go to bed. After that everything started to fall into place. We chose our style of clothing; we chose our friends; we chose our way of life. In many aspects of life, the choice is ours, and we either blossom in the fruits of those choices or suffer their consequences.

Today's readings are about choices placed by God before the people. In the passage from Deuteronomy, Moses enjoins the people to internalize the laws of God, to take them into their minds and hearts, to make them the standards by which they live their lives. He then directs them to "bind them at your wrist as a sign, and let them be a pendant on your forehead." This custom of carrying passages of the law on one's person, the origin of the practice of wearing phylacteries, was meant to remind one of the importance of the law in all the circumstances of life.

In words that are straightforward and unembellished, Moses then described two possible attitudes toward the commandments. The people could decide either to follow the direction set by the commandments and enjoy the resulting blessings, or to reject the laws and place themselves in grave peril. Regardless of the seriousness of this situation, God did not force the people to decide one way or the other. They knew that either blessing or curse was attendant on their choice, but that choice was still theirs to make. The responsorial psalm shows that a similar choice was placed before the psalmist. Having chosen in favor of God, the psalmist looked forward to the blessings of deliverance and the security that fidelity to God promised.

Jesus held out options to his disciples as well. They could either accept his teaching and act on it, or they could refuse to listen to him and continue to live as they had been living. Jesus' teachings were not merely captivating words that thrilled and inspired; they were challenges. They consisted of more than delightful nouns and colorful adjectives. One might say that they were more like imperative verbs, demanding action. This fact is made clear in the passage for today's Gospel: "Not everyone who says to me, 'Lord, Lord,' will enter the kingdom of heaven, but only the one who does the will of my Father in heaven." To put it another way, "Actions speak louder than words." Jesus was not here suggesting that professions of faith are not important and good works alone are what count. Rather, he insisted that those who profess faith but do not put that faith into action are like people who build a house on sand. Just as such a house will not endure, so pious but empty words will not stand.

But those whom Jesus criticized had not sat by idly, doing nothing. Many of them had driven out demons and performed mighty deeds in Jesus' own name. Why did he respond to them with such harsh words: "I never knew you. Depart from me, you evildoers"? Could it be that theirs was a superficial discipleship, that they had been seduced by their ability to perform ostentatious deeds rather than devoted to doing God's will?

Jesus' thinking here may sound contradictory to Paul's message as found in the second reading. There he maintains that we are "justified by faith apart from the works of the law." Is there really a contradiction here? Was Jesus insisting on works over faith, and Paul on faith over works? Not at all! Each one was speaking to the particular situation of his time, and the two situations were very different. Jesus was criticizing those whose faith was not the driving force in their lives. They may have recognized him as "Lord" and even performed extraordinary deeds, but their actions did not conform to or flow from an expression of faith. Using the phylacteries as an example, we might say that they wore the phylacteries in public without having taken the law into their minds and hearts. On the other hand, Paul was talking to people who believed that conformity to the law and not faith in Jesus made them righteous in the eyes of God. Using the image of the phylacteries again, we might say that the people in Paul's audience may have thought that wearing phylacteries was all that was necessary. Jesus called for faith in action; Paul insisted that good works must flow from faith, not replace it.

Similar choices are set before us today. Do we call ourselves Christian, yet live according to the standards of a godless society? Do we think our observance of religious customs is enough? Or, have we listened to the words of Jesus and acted on them?

Praying with Scripture

- What are some of the major choices you have made in your life?

- In what ways have these choices enhanced your life and the lives of others?

- Which choices might you have to reconsider?

TENTH SUNDAY IN ORDINARY TIME

Readings:
Hos 6:3-6; Ps 50:1, 8, 12-15;
Rom 4:18-25; Matt 9:9-13

LOVE MAKES THE WORLD GO 'ROUND!

We are bombarded with talk of love. Advertisements capitalize on it with inspiring scenes and gestures; music extols its virtues; and greeting cards convey tender sentiments. Despite this, there seems to be so little genuine love in the world. Perhaps this is because we do not think that some people have earned our love. How can we be expected to love people who do not seem to have our best interests at heart? Even our friends and family members are often fickle and unreliable. Do such people deserve our love?

The picture is not totally bleak. We all know of people whose love for another cannot be questioned. Parents often continue to make sacrifices for children who are ungrateful. Wives and husbands care tenderly for stricken spouses who show no signs of improvement. We all know selfless neighbors, teachers, and church personnel. The world is not devoid of genuine love.

The nature imagery, found in the passage from Hosea, that characterizes God's care of the people is striking in its tenderness. The first light of dawn is always filled with promise. Darkness and the fear that invade it lose their hold, and new possibilities accompany the new light. Spring rain has life-giving properties. It waters the earth and quenches the thirst of living creatures. It is no wonder the ancients characterized their creator-god as a storm deity. Lest we lose ourselves in the beauty of this poetry, we should not forget that this divine tenderness and care are lavished on people whose "piety is like a morning cloud, like dew that early passes away." In other words, the heat of the day dissipates it. Such piety is certainly fickle and unreliable. Such devotion does not earn God's care.

God's next words are alarming: "For this reason I smote them through the prophets, I slew them by the words of my mouth." God is not happy with superficial piety, devotion that vanishes in the heat of life. What does God ask of us? Piety that is grounded in genuine love. It is not enough to offer sacrifice; it is not enough to fulfill one's "Sunday obligation." The psalm response emphasizes this. God does not need our sacrifices or holocausts. Instead, God desires genuine love. The Hebrew word used by Hosea is *chesed*, the steadfast loving-kindness that is associated with covenant commitment.

The gospel reading illustrates this same theme. Matthew was a customs officer, a Jew hired by the hated Roman occupiers who usually sat at borders collecting taxes on goods in transit. Since tax collectors were not generally salaried, their livelihood came from what they could exact from people over and above the required taxes. Matthew was not the kind of man the Jewish populace would trust, much less admire. His occupation marked him as a sinner. Yet, he was called by Jesus to follow him. In fact, Jesus even entered the house of this sinner and shared a meal with him. What had Matthew done to deserve such an honor? Nothing.

When the self-righteous expressed their disdain to the disciples, Jesus replied, "I desire mercy, not sacrifice." It is true that Matthew had not earned the privilege of being called by Jesus. He was, in fact, in need of the care that only Jesus could give. The mercy of which Jesus spoke is also associated with covenant commitment.

These two readings point to the undeserved love and mercy that God desires to *bestow on us*. However, here the love and mercy are what God *expects of us*. These readings present us with a double challenge. First, they call us to the realization that we cannot earn God's love and mercy. Since we live in societies that are often governed by some form of merit system, this is a difficult lesson to learn. It is a hard lesson in humility. Second, the readings tell us that such love and mercy are required of us as well. Our piety must be rooted deeply in covenant commitment, not merely in external practices, and we must be merciful in our dealings with others.

These two readings point to yet another issue, namely, the unacceptability of merely external practices. It is clear that the people at the time of Hosea offered sacrifices and holocausts to God. They may have even believed that these fulfilled their obligation. But they did not. At the time of Jesus, the Pharisees were recognized interpreters of the faith. Their condemnation of Jesus' association with tax collectors and sinners suggests that, in their view, their own observance of law and custom made them righteous in the eyes of God. But it did not. External observance, as important as it certainly is, cannot compare to the genuine love and mercy required of disciples of Jesus. It is this kind of love that really makes the world go 'round.

Praying with Scripture

- Reflect on the ways that you have known God's love and mercy.

- Is your love narrowly restricted to those who already love you?

- How might you bestow such love on others?

ELEVENTH SUNDAY IN ORDINARY TIME
Readings:
Exod 19:2–6a; Ps 100:1–3, 5;
Rom 5:6–11; Matt 9:36—10:8

You Are the One I Choose

"You're my best friend!" "You're my favorite teacher!" "I love you more than anyone else in the world!" Who does not appreciate hearing sentiments like these expressed? They tell us that we are special to someone; they indicate that our particular uniqueness is recognized and valued by another. They are not merely flattering; they bolster our sense of ourselves.

In the first reading for today, God assures the Israelites that they are extraordinary: "You are my special possession, dearer to me than all other people." This claim has bothered non-Israelites down through the ages. Did God really single one nation out of all the nations of the world? And if so, is that fair? Or does this bold claim come from the Israelites themselves? And if it does, what has given them the right to make it?

Again and again, the Israelites did maintain that they were God's chosen people. Such a claim does not sound so arrogant when we realize that many peoples throughout the ancient world worshiped their own patron god and made this claim in relation to that god. The claim takes on a different tenor, however, when people believe that there is only one God, and that this one God has singled out one nation.

We must remember that a displaced people who had only recently been delivered from the oppressive control of a much stronger nation made the claim. Under these circumstances, it almost seems ludicrous for the Israelites to make such a bold claim. Why would God care about a ragtag group of escaped slaves? But this is precisely the point of the reading. It is not that the Israelites were better because they were chosen, but that God chose people who were vulnerable. This fact significantly refocuses their claim of having been specially chosen by God. It says more about God than it does about Israel itself. It says that God is particularly concerned about the weak and the lowly, the underprivileged and the dispossessed, those who may not be able to make it in the world on their own. This may be a bold claim, but is it an arrogant one?

The people described in the Gospel are also vulnerable; "they were troubled and abandoned, like sheep without a shepherd." Jesus "was moved with pity for them," and for their sake he sent the Twelve "to drive [unclean spirits] out and to cure every disease and every illness." These miraculous feats were considered signs of the advent of the reign of God, that time of fulfillment when blessings would triumph over hardships. We should note that Jesus was moved to pity, but it was the disciples who performed the deeds of mercy.

Jesus was certainly compassionate, but his concern for the needy was not simply the touching human sentiment we too might experience when we come upon undeserved misfortune. His compassion was grounded in the covenant. Traces of this covenant theology are present in the psalm response where the shepherd theme is coupled with technical covenant language—"kindness" and "faithfulness." There we see that the care the shepherd shows the sheep stems from the covenant bond that binds them together. As moving as such scenes of compassion might be, they still do not explain why God seems to choose for consideration people whom society considers to be "losers."

God made the covenant with the entire community of Israel, not merely with a few chosen individuals like Abraham or Moses. According to covenant ideology in ancient Near Eastern thinking, the human partners in the covenant were bound to each other as well as to God. Consequently, the covenant carried communal responsibilities. Therefore, if the community failed in any way to care for its needy and vulnerable members, God, as a both faithful and magnanimous covenant partner, would side with those who had been neglected or oppressed. This explains why God always seemed to be on the side of the vulnerable. It was not because they were better than others, but it was because the rest of the community had not addressed their needs. Today, this same concern is captured by the expression "preferential option for the poor." We too are called to stand with the needy, not because we are sensitive and generous, but because it is our responsibility as people in covenant with God and with them.

Paul treats the graciousness of God from a slightly different perspective. He does not address political or social vulnerability, but speaks of the helplessness that results from human sinfulness. We did not merit God's favor. Despite this, "while we were still sinners, Christ died for us." Like the ancient Israelites before us, and the troubled people at the time of Jesus, we are the undeserving recipients of God's graciousness.

Praying with Scripture

- In what ways have you been the recipient of God's graciousness?

- Spend time today thanking God for providing you with what you need.

- How might you be the agent through whom God blesses others?

TWELFTH SUNDAY IN ORDINARY TIME
Readings:
*Jer 20:10–13; Ps 69:8–10, 14, 17, 33–35;
Rom 5:12–15; Matt 10:26–33*

STAND FIRM!

The response of the world at the death and funeral of Pope John Paul II was a sight to behold. Throngs of people of every religious affiliation gathered in Rome and in cities all over the world to show their respect for this very popular, world-traveling pontiff. Particularly obvious was the participation of crowds of young people. Why was this man so loved? These throngs of people may not have followed all the moral directives the pope had issued during his long pontificate, nor might they have agreed with all his doctrinal teachings. This outpouring of support and emotion was not simply an expression of pity for an old man whose painful diminishment made public was now ended, for John Paul II attracted crowds throughout his entire reign. What was it about this man that captured the imagination of so many and drew him into the embrace of their affection?

In a world that has witnessed so much deceit, manipulation, and violence in its political and religious leaders, John Paul II was seen by all as a man of unquestionable integrity. One might disagree with him on many fronts, but his fundamental uprightness was never questioned. Insistence on the innate God-given dignity of all women and men, not personal gain, was the wellspring of his life. People the world over found in him the integrity for which they longed. One cannot help asking, "Why does there seem to be so little integrity in the world today?" Perhaps it is because of the price that such integrity exacts.

Today's readings offer us examples of this kind of integrity, the cost one might be asked to pay because of it, and the source of strength needed to be faithful to one's commitment. Jeremiah's prophetic message of condemnation was met with resistance from both the political and the religious officials of his day. Even those he considered his friends turned against him. His very life was in jeopardy. Still, he was not deterred from his commitment. Rather, he relied on God alone. This is seen in his words: "The LORD is with me like a mighty champion." Confident that God would intervene, Jeremiah remained steadfast in the face of bitter persecution. And what had been the cause of the resentment against and persecution of the prophet? He had proclaimed God's call for repentance to a sinful people. In their eyes, Jeremiah was the enemy; in God's eyes, he was a faithful servant.

The responsorial psalm picks up many of the same themes. It acknowledges that God's righteous ones often face insult because of their commitment, and sometimes this comes even from those persons who are closest to them. However, they should be confident that God knows their plight and will deliver them from their misfortune.

In the Gospel we see Jesus exhorting his disciples to stand firm in the face of similar persecution. He tells them to proclaim the gospel fearlessly despite the unpopularity of the message, and to acknowledge their commitment to him regardless of the price they may have to pay for their steadfastness. Their fidelity placed their lives in jeopardy, just as had been the case with Jeremiah. However, Jesus promises them that, even though they may have to endure physical suffering, God will certainly care for them. He utilizes imagery from the world of nature to illustrate the providence of God. The omnipotent Creator-God is aware of every detail of the natural world. Not even the fate of simple sparrows goes unnoticed. "So, do not be afraid; you are worth more than many sparrows." Such encouragement was meant to strengthen their resolve to stand firm in their commitment, even in the face of extraordinary tribulation.

When we are overwhelmed by the difficulty that steadfastness to the call of God may entail, we need only turn to Paul's message in the second reading. There he declares that the grace of God that is at our disposal far outstrips anything that might oppose it. Jesus procured this grace for us. This is why it will endure and will provide us with the strength and solace we need to face the hardships that life might thrust upon us.

Few of us will ever find ourselves on the world stage as was John Paul II or Jeremiah, or even as were the first disciples. However, we are all called upon to acknowledge our Christian discipleship through the respect we show to others, the honesty of our dealings with them, and the unselfishness of our lives. In so many ways, our society seems to disdain such values. It even ridicules those who stand for them. Still, this is the kind of integrity expected of all of us. It is imperative that we nurture it in our lives, for our world is in desperate need of it!

Praying with Scripture

- Who are your heroes? What makes them heroes?

- When have you proclaimed the gospel fearlessly?

- In what ways are you called to live life with integrity?

THIRTEENTH SUNDAY IN ORDINARY TIME
Readings:
2 Kgs 4:8–11, 14–16a; Ps 89:2–3, 16–19; Rom 6:3–4, 8–11; Matt 10:37–42

OPENHEARTED HOSPITALITY

In the ancient world, hospitality was not merely a point of etiquette; it was a requirement for survival in a perilous world. There were no general stores or trading posts and so travelers depended upon the goodwill of others for food, shelter, and necessary supplies while they were on a journey. The custom assured strangers that they would not be exploited as long as they themselves posed no threat. Some people even believed that divine beings roamed the earth in search of examples of human graciousness: "Do not neglect hospitality, for through it some unknowingly entertained angels" (Heb 13:2).

Today's readings include examples of ancient hospitality. They also mention the rewards that accrue from the practice of it. The reading from 2 Kings describes the openness of a Shunammite woman. She is a woman of influence, a very unusual characteristic for a woman in an ancient patriarchal society. However, since her husband was "getting on in years," she may have been experienced in caring for needy men. She is the one who urged Elisha to dine with her and who arranged a little room on the roof where he would always be welcome. In gratitude for this hospitality, Elisha promised that she would have a son. This promise was not merely a gesture of gratitude. A son would eventually inherit family property and would care for the woman as she herself aged. She provided for the prophet; he, in turn, provided for her.

We find this same theme in the Gospel. There we see Jesus instructing his followers on the need for hospitality, but it is hospitality from a particular point of view. The woman in the first reading is the one who opens her home. Jesus is talking about openhearted hospitality extended to apostles as ministers of the gospel. As representatives of Jesus, they are told, "Who receives you receives me." The hospitality spoken of here is more than the ancient custom that was so necessary for survival in a perilous world. The ancient traveler was certainly exposed to danger, but the ministers of the gospel were doubly defenseless. They deliberately made themselves vulnerable by dissociating themselves from family support and by accepting hardship for the sake of the gospel. Jesus declares that whoever does the slightest favor for them, even giving them a cup of cold water, will be rewarded.

We must be careful that we not take this teaching too literally, lest we perform acts of kindness simply for the compensation we think should be our due. We are called to be openhearted in our service out of a sense of hospitality, not for the sake of reward. It should be noted that Jesus does not really describe this reward.

It may, in fact, come as a surprise. Jesus merely says that acts of kindness or hospitality will not go unrequited.

The "little ones" of whom Jesus spoke were probably disciples, not children. Jesus lived in a world in which one's worth was determined by one's social status. This social class could be either inherited or earned. However, it could also be lost through behavior that might disgrace the head of the family. Such behavior included loss of money, serious hardship, or dishonorable family members. These were all situations indicating that the head of the family, the patriarch, was unable to exercise control over his own world. In a society governed by principles of honor and shame, as were most societies in the ancient world, men were always vying for more honor, and the rest of the household was held in check lest they bring shame to the householder. Jesus did not want his disciples caught up in such competitive concerns. His followers were to be unassuming, like unimportant children. It is of them that Jesus says, "Whoever receives you receives me, and whoever receives me receives the one who sent me."

This practice of ministerial hospitality in no way suggests that the life of the disciples was easy. They may have been assured of the generosity of others ("The laborer deserves to be paid," Luke 10:7; 1 Tim 5:18), but they were required to make great sacrifices. They had to be willing even to sever intimate family ties, if called upon to do so. And as if this were not sacrifice enough, they were promised the cross.

Today's followers of Jesus are certainly promised a reward. Paul tells us that we are called to "live in newness of life." However, this privilege is extended to us because "we were baptized into his death." Baptism has made us new people. We are now people whose value is not determined by social status. We are people who extend openhearted Christian hospitality to others, knowing that it is not merely angels whom we might be entertaining. Rather, it is Jesus himself, along with the one who sent him.

Praying with Scripture

- Who in your acquaintance extends openhearted hospitality to others? What might you learn from them?

- What might you do to extend some form of hospitality to needy people in your community?

- How supportive are you of those who have dedicated their lives to the spread of the gospel?

FOURTEENTH SUNDAY IN ORDINARY TIME
Readings:
Zech 9:9–10; Ps 145:1–2, 8–11, 13–14;
Rom 8:9, 11–13; Matt 11:25–30

THREE CHEERS FOR GOD!

Although it is not Trinity Sunday, the readings for today invite us to reflect on the mystery of our triune God and on the way of living to which intimacy with God calls us. It is really the psalm that sets the stage for our reflections today. It summons us to praise God for the goodness shown us: "The LORD is gracious and merciful, slow to anger and of great kindness."

This description of God follows the account of the ancient Israelites' sin of worshiping the golden calf (Exod 34:6). The description, which contains the technical covenant language of mercy and loving-kindness, is extraordinary when we remember that God is revealed in this way to an apostate people. They had just been delivered from Egyptian bondage, and had entered into a solemn covenant with God, promising to be a faithful partner. Impatient with Moses' absence, they turned to the image of a golden calf. This short verse concisely characterizes the essence of our God. It reminds us that God is not primarily a judge who punishes disloyalty, nor even one whose priority is rewarding goodness. Our God knows human frailty and is always ready to show mercy.

This is the God whom Jesus calls "Father," the Lord of heaven and earth. The "Father-Son" language in the Gospel points to the intimate bond that unites them: "No one knows the Father except the Son, and no one knows the Son except the Father." Despite this exclusive intimacy, Jesus is willing to reveal his Father to his disciples and to us. Thus, it is through Jesus that we come to know the gracious and merciful God who gave the ancient Israelites a second chance.

The Gospel discloses another characteristic of this God, namely, God's preference for those who are insignificant. This was certainly true of the Israelites, and it is the case here as well. The wise and the learned, the influential members of society, are not the ones to whom the secret mysteries of God are revealed. Rather, they are disclosed to the little ones. While the word can mean "children," it probably refers to the insignificant ones. This interpretation is borne out in the second part of the reading where Jesus directs his followers to be meek and humble of heart, hardly characteristics of those who arrogantly consider themselves of great consequence. In contrast to this, the followers of Jesus are invited to consider themselves insignificant according to worldly standards. Yoke frequently suggests some form of submission. However, "yoke of the law" was a common expression for rabbinic teaching. This is probably how yoke is used here. In other words, when Jesus instructs his disciples to "learn from me," he is inviting them to take upon themselves the "yoke" of his teachings.

Though life in the Spirit is the primary focus of Paul's message, he does direct our attention to the relationship between Jesus and the Spirit of God. It is this Spirit who raised Jesus from the dead. It is this same Spirit who dwells in us, enabling us to live transformed lives. These readings portray Jesus as a kind of intermediary between us and both the Father and the Spirit. He reveals his Father to us, and he shares his Spirit with us.

If, as the psalm response states, we are in a covenant relationship with God, what is required of us? What dispositions are appropriate for covenant partners? Principally, we are exhorted to be meek and humble of heart, as Jesus was. How puzzling! The one who alone knows God and whose Spirit enlivens the dead is meek and humble of heart. Not only is God gracious and merciful, as the psalm tells us, but God works through those who are meek and humble. We see this in the first reading as well. The mysterious royal figure of the future will come riding on the lowly ass of the simple people, not on the magnificent stallion of the conqueror. War and the weapons of war will be abolished and he will come to establish peace, not only for a united Israel, but for all of the nations as well. His reign of peace will extend to the entire world, "from sea to sea, and from the River to the ends of the earth."

These vignettes do not deny the power and might of God. They suggest, instead, that this power and might reside precisely in attributes of graciousness and mercy, meekness and humility. The Gospel calls us to imitate these dispositions. We will be like Jesus, whose very being reveals God to us, when we too are gracious and merciful, meek and humble of heart. As difficult as this manner of living may be, we have the power of the Spirit dwelling within us, so that we can truly live transformed lives.

Praying with Scripture

- Reflect on the times when you have experienced the mercy of God as conveyed to you through the mercy of others.

- What aspects of the teaching of Jesus do you find the hardest to bear? Pray for the grace to be faithful in these areas.

- Make the responsorial psalm your prayer today, being grateful for God's kindness to you.

FIFTEENTH SUNDAY IN ORDINARY TIME
Readings:
Isa 55:10–11; Ps 65:10–14; Rom 8:18–23; Matt 13:1–23

WHAT A WONDERFUL WORLD!

Several years ago, jazz musician Louie Armstrong was inspired by the magnificence of the natural world as he sang of the tenderness of human love. Moved by the luxurious green of trees, the vibrant red of roses, the soothing blue of the sky, the brightness of day and the sacredness of night, all he could exclaim was: "What a wonderful world!"

The beauty of the world also enthralled the biblical authors of today's readings. They employed natural imagery to speak of God and the things of God. Isaiah was in awe of the fructifying potential of the rain as he sang the praises of God's word. The psalmist painted scenes of the life-giving world when proclaiming the glories of salvation. Paul likened our longing for redemption to Creation's struggle to bring forth new life. Finally, Jesus compared various degrees of openness to the word of God with different kinds of ground. The natural world does indeed lend itself to lessons about God.

How does this imagery work? Metaphors use a well-known characteristic of one reality to throw light on a lesser-known second reality. For example, we use our experience of rainfall and the natural abundance that it yields to throw light on the life-giving capacity of God's word. Or, our knowledge of the difference between fertile soil and land that produces only thorns is used to explain various degrees of openness to allowing that same word to take root and flourish in our lives. It is because we are so familiar with natural creation that we are able to appreciate metaphors like these that speak of the mysterious ways of God.

What does this imagery mean? The marvelous cycle of rainfall, evaporation, and then atmospheric condensation is an apt image of the indefatigable power of God's word, as found in the first reading: "[M]y word shall not return to me void." Water's ability to effect vegetation never ceased to mystify the ancient people. They were so entranced by this power that they often regarded water as a divine force that impregnated the earth. The life-giving potential of that same word is captured in Jesus' parable as well. There, however, the focus is on the quality of the land and its ability to bring forth life. Earth's never-ending fecundity was also considered by some to be divine. Earth was seen as the divine mother who brought forth all living beings. Neither the prophet Isaiah nor Jesus actually believed that these natural elements were divine. However, both of them used nature's remarkable abilities to make some point about the marvels of the word of God.

What message concerning God's word do these nature metaphors intend to communicate? The Isaian passage emphasizes the unflagging power of that word. It almost suggests that nothing can stop it from accomplishing its end. The positive imagery employed indicates that this is an oracle of salvation and therefore would have been a very consoling message for people who were in the throes of suffering. It assured them that God's promise of blessing would not be deterred. The Gospel does not deny this power, but it insists that the fruitfulness of the yield depends on the quality of the soil. The yield may be thirty, sixty, or hundredfold. In other words, the effectiveness of God's word is determined by our openness to that word. Employing the metaphor in examining the responsorial psalm, one might say that the rich harvest depicted there could signify a truly fruitful life. But then, it is up to us to decide which kind of soil we are.

There must be a common characteristic for the metaphor to be meaningful, and here is where natural metaphors are particularly challenging today. How will we use them to speak of God's ways in our lives if features of our world no longer correspond with divine attributes? Would Isaiah compare God's word with acid rain? How would the psalmist praise God if the earth were unable to bring forth healthful food? Would Jesus' sower cast the seed onto land that is polluted? Today we have to wonder: Is creation groaning with the labor pangs of new life, as Paul suggested, or with the cancer of contamination?

These readings should remind us that we are natural creatures and everything about us is a part of the natural world or is mediated to us through that world. This is true even of our understanding of God. The world is not ours; we only hold it in trust. Like the rest of earth's living creatures, we are dependent on the rain. We come from the earth as from a mother, and we are nourished from this same source of life. These readings remind us that it is truly a wonderful world!

Praying with Scripture

- Spend some time absorbing the beauty of the natural world and thanking God for it.

- Choose one concrete action that might enhance your environment.

- In what ways might you be resistant to the message of this Sunday's readings?

SIXTEENTH SUNDAY IN ORDINARY TIME
Readings:
Wis 12:13, 16–19; Ps 86:5–6, 9–10, 15–16;
Rom 8:26–27; Matt 13:24–43

NOTHING'S PERFECT!

One of the great disappointments of my life was the painful realization that every religious group to which I belong is imperfect. This should not have surprised me. Religious or not, each group is made up of limited human beings. Still, idealistic as I was, I expected more of religious people. But then, what right did I have to point a finger at others? My own limitations should have given me some insight into this matter.

I am not the only person who has been disappointed in this way. We all know good, sincere people who have left the church because they are disappointed with some of its members. They are offended by poor liturgies or uninspiring preaching; they can no longer abide the sexism or racism that grips so many; they are disillusioned by the disregard of the privileged for the vulnerable and needy of the world; they are horrified by the abuse of power and authority. They maintain that the church should be above such misconduct.

There certainly are many people within the church who stand in opposition to such evils and who do what they can to eliminate them. Still, the church is not perfect; nothing made up of limited human beings is. And in our own ways, we all contribute to this lack of perfection. This is no excuse for wrongdoing; it is simply a statement of fact. To use vocabulary from New Testament theology, the reign of God is "already-but-not-yet" holy. The Second Vatican Council clearly identified the church as "on earth, the seed and the beginning of that kingdom. While it slowly grows to maturity, the church longs for the completed kingdom." Hence, the church shares this same incompleteness. (Such a precise distinction between the church and the reign of God is not made in these metaphorical parables.)

Jesus was well aware of this very human condition among his own disciples. We see this in the parable he taught in today's Gospel. The field (the reign of God) contains both wheat and weeds. Our inclination might be to rid the field of those whom we consider undesirable. Jesus insists: "No!" In our zeal to uproot what we think is bad, we might uproot what is really good. Besides, who determines which is bad and which is good? Dishonorable people have often been thought to be righteous, while the truly righteous frequently have been overlooked, rejected, or even condemned. Furthermore, there is always the possibility of conversion. Had the church been too quick to weed out sinners from its midst it might never have been enriched by a Charles de Foucauld or an Augustine of Hippo, or even a Simon Peter. Until the time of harvest, when the final day of eschatological fulfillment dawns, we will always be a church that is an assemblage of sinners, ourselves among them.

In the meantime, how are we supposed to live in the church with such a mix of people? Both the first reading and the gospel passage provide us with guidelines. The passage from Wisdom is simple and to the point: "[T]hose who are just must be kind." The two remaining parables in the Gospel also offer insights into appropriate behavior for those who would belong to the reign of God. The parable of the mustard seed speaks about inclusivity. We all have a tendency to embrace only certain groups of people and to dismiss others. While the inclination itself may be innocent, it can often develop into destructive prejudice and discrimination. By characterizing the church as a large plant in whose branches various birds can find a dwelling, it teaches us to overcome our gender, racial, ethnic, economic, and any other form of bias in order to make room for all people. The parable of the yeast prompts us to lose ourselves, our selfishness and pettiness, in order that the community might be transformed into something that is life-giving. Aware of our own human limitations, we might fear that we do not have what it takes to meet these challenges. At such times we should take to heart Paul's message found in the second reading: "The Spirit comes to the aid of our weakness."

It is precisely through the give-and-take of life with selfish, inconsiderate sinners like ourselves that we learn to be patient and understanding, tolerant and forgiving. If we allow the grace of God to work in our lives, it can both refine and strengthen us. We cannot deny that some people do indeed offend us, but the very same people can encourage and inspire us as well. Today's reading from Wisdom assures us that we are God's people, cared for and purified by God. The Gospel reminds us that it is God's church destined for that final kingdom where "the righteous will shine like the sun."

Praying with Scripture

- What are you doing to make the church holier?

- How open is your parish church to diversity? What might you do to improve it?

- Pray for the conversion of someone whom you consider a sinner.

SEVENTEENTH SUNDAY IN ORDINARY TIME
Readings:
1 Kgs 3:5, 7–12; Ps 119:57, 72, 76–77, 127–130; Rom 8:28–30; Matt 13:44–52

THE PEARL OF GREAT PRICE

If God approached you, as he did Solomon, and said, "Ask something of me and I will give it to you," how would you respond?

Would you ask for money? A happy family? Good health? World peace? Solomon asked for "an understanding heart to judge your people and to distinguish right from wrong." Without minimizing the selfless character of his request, we should remember that, as king, he had no need of more riches. However, he certainly could have asked for a more expansive kingdom, a better economy, or even revenge on his enemies. Instead, he asked for the disposition needed to serve his people well. Whether this actually happened or not, the account does pose an interesting question. How would you respond?

What is it that we ask of God? I doubt that I am the only one who, sometime in life, prayed to pass a test, or for good picnic weather, or to be chosen for what I might have considered an honor. As important as such prayers might have seemed at the moment, if I were to be honest with myself, I would have to admit that they were certainly quite trivial when you look at the whole scheme of things. But then, to what extent do we really know what counts in life? It takes great insight to realize what it is we should treasure in life and what is not worthy of us. This is particularly difficult when society assaults us with values that are really dis-values. Perhaps we should all pray for "an understanding heart."

Today's Gospel contains three parables, three wisdom stories that provide glimpses into the nature of the reign of heaven. The first two lend themselves to this particular reflection. The metaphors of the treasure in the field and the pearl of great price point to the inestimable value of the reign of God. Who wouldn't be willing to give up all else in order to attain the treasure or the pearl? Even reading the parables literally, we know that these are complicated situations. How did the person know that the treasure or the pearl were there in the first place? And what if that person did not have enough resources to make the sale? In other words, we need attentiveness to discover the treasures, insight to realize that they are worth everything else we might possess and more, and enough courage to make the changes required for obtaining what we desire. How do we stand in this regard? Do we consider the kingdom worth the effort?

What is this reign of heaven for which we should be willing to give up all else? It is a way of living life here and now, not merely a state of being that will unfold after death. It is a life of faithful commitment; it is a life of integrity, of trust in God and service of others. It is the kind of life Solomon wanted for his people, a life that can distinguish right from wrong. It is the kind of life that the psalmist sought—a life lived in harmony with the law. Paul describes this life as one lived in conformity to the image of God's own Son. One cannot help but ask a further question: If we are finally able to acquire the treasure or the pearl, do we hug it to ourselves, thinking that it is ours and ours alone? Or are we like Solomon, who thought that the only real treasure was unselfish service to others?

Paul further states that God foreknew, then predestined, then called, justified, and glorified those committed to live in this way. This passage has troubled many people down through the ages. We do not usually have difficulty understanding what is meant when we say that God called, justified, and glorified. We are probably not even bothered with the idea of divine fore-knowledge. It is with the notion of predestination that we some-times struggle. Predestination does not mean, however, that only some were chosen to be saved and some were not. We are accus-tomed to the idea that *all* are foreknown by God. Paul is very clear that God's call is made to *all*. Therefore, we can rightly conclude that *all* those called and foreknown are "predestined to be con-formed to the image of [God's] Son." In other words, all people are meant to be justified and glorified; all people are given the oppor-tunity to discover the treasure buried in the field or the pearl of great price; all people are prompted to sell what they have in order to acquire the fortune. The cost may be great. The parable sug-gests that we will have to give up everything else. Paul reminds us, however, that "all things work for good for those who love God."

Praying with Scripture

- What in your life do you consider the "pearl of great price"? Is it enduring?

- What sacrifices are you willing to make for the kingdom of God?

- Pray for insight to recognize what is truly valuable and the courage to pursue it.

EIGHTEENTH SUNDAY IN ORDINARY TIME
Readings:
Isa 55:1–3; Ps 145:8–9, 15–18;
Rom 8:35, 37–39; Matt 14:13–21

SIT DOWN AND EAT!

It is very convenient nowadays to drive up to a squawking metal box, place an order for food, turn the corner of the building, and pick up a meal in a colorfully decorated box or bag. However, our penchant for quick convenience is often bought at the price of genuine human sharing. There is something very intimate about eating with another person. It is more than merely assuaging one's hunger for food and quenching one's thirst. Sharing a meal satisfies the hunger for human contact and interaction. It bespeaks friendship and respect, even love. Families celebrate birthdays and holidays around a table sumptuously laden with appetizing food; friends enjoy each other's company and exchange intimacies over a meal; and people from all walks of life are honored at banquets. There is more than eating that goes on at the table.

The reading from the prophet Isaiah employs the metaphor of a meal to point to something much deeper than human celebration and bonding. There we find God offering the people of Israel the rich fare of a lavish banquet. Originally this oracle envisioned a future in which the poor would enjoy the luxurious fruits of the land. This theme is supported by the responsorial psalm, which states, "The eyes of all look hopefully to you, and you give them their food in due season." The covenant once made exclusively with David and his royal descendants is democratized in the Isaian passage. The blessings of the land, which are really the blessings of God, are there offered to those who would not otherwise be able to afford them. Though the poetry invites these people to enjoy food and drink, the real invitation is to covenant participation.

The Gospel reports another kind of meal. This account has links to a similar episode in the life of the prophet Elisha (cf. 2 Kgs 4:42-44), and this similarity would not have been lost on the followers of Jesus. The details of the story sketch a dramatic event. As mentioned above, though spectacular, the event was not unique in the history of Israel. Furthermore, the words, "he said the blessing, broke the loaves, and gave them to the disciples," were words commonly used at Jewish meals. They took on added meaning in the Christian community, however, for they became part of a eucharistic formula, as found in Matthew's gospel account (cf. Matt 26:26–27)..Furthermore, as in the passage from Isaiah read today, the eschatological time of fulfillment was often characterized as a bountiful banquet. It is easy to see that this account of Jesus' feeding the multitude contains both eucharistic and eschatological features, suggesting that it is more than a story of the miraculous multiplication of bread.

Ancient Jewish apocalyptic lore maintained that the evil forces of chaos defeated during the primeval cosmic battle would constitute the fare served at the eschatological banquet. These beasts were the sea monsters Behemoth (cf. Job 40:15) and Leviathan (cf. Job 41:1; Ps 104:26). Is it merely coincidence that this gospel narrative, with its eschatological nuance, adds two fish to the desert menu? It seems that this story can boast three levels of meaning. The obvious one is an account of a wondrous feeding of hungry people in the wilderness. On a second level we can discern a foreshadowing of the Eucharist. Finally, there is a promise of eschatological fulfillment.

The meals depicted in these readings were not fast-food pick-ups. They were communal sharings. We see this clearly in the invitation extended in the first reading: "All you...come...!" Such open-ended invitations are bound to attract all sorts of people, some whom we would be proud to include at our table, others we would prefer to rule out. Furthermore, the meal was a celebration of covenant union. It was not a human banquet to which God was invited; rather, it was God's banquet to which humans were invited. The multiplication of the loaves and the fishes that unfolds in the Gospel was not only a communal meal, but it also included communal ministry. Jesus' disciples both distributed the food and collected the fragments that were left over.

What might these readings have to say to us today? They certainly reinforce our teaching on the eschatological dimension of every Eucharist: "As often as you eat this bread and drink the cup, you proclaim the death of the Lord until he comes" (1 Cor 11:26). They might also prompt us to cherish the meals we share with those we love. Such meals may not be eucharistic sacraments, but they certainly can be sacramental eucharists, meals of thanksgiving. Finally, they challenge us to be active participants in the Eucharist. This does not simply mean that we join in the prayers and the singing during the ritual celebration. It means that, as true disciples of Jesus, we are actively involved in meeting the needs of others.

Praying with Scripture

- What might you do to make meals with family and friends more meaningful experiences?

- Perform one act that will alleviate the hunger of another.

- Pray for the grace to realize the eschatological significance of the Eucharist.

NINETEENTH SUNDAY IN ORDINARY TIME
Readings:
1 Kgs 19:9a, 11–13a; Ps 85:9–14; Rom 9:1–5; Matt 14:22–33

JUST WHAT DOES GOD EXPECT OF US?

Is it true that life becomes increasingly difficult over the years? Or might it be that we have simply grown up and we now realize that it has always been a challenge and we were simply shielded from its hardships? We were taught to live good lives, to be kind to others, and to follow the rules. Why is it, then, that the more we try to live lives of integrity and generosity, the harder life seems to be? Just what does God expect of us? Perhaps this is the wrong question. Perhaps we should ask, "Just what do we expect of God?"

Today's readings challenge some of the expectations we might have of life or of God. In the first account we see that Elijah had unrealistic expectations of God. He seems to have presumed that a genuine experience of God would be accompanied by extraordinary phenomena. After all, God spoke to Job out of a mighty wind (Job 38:1); an earthquake occurred when God delivered the commandments to Moses (Exod 19:18); finally, God called Moses from the midst of a burning bush (Exod 3:2). Since such were customary ways that God communicated with human beings, some wondrous natural phenomenon would certainly announce and accompany God's manifestation to Elijah. But no! God was in no such extraordinary occurrence. Rather, it was in the tiny whispering sound that Elijah recognized the presence of God.

In its own way, this short passage alerts us to the mysterious workings of God in two ways. First, it cautions us not to think that we understand the ways of God. When we do, we are often inclined to presume to plan the path along which God will travel. Second, if we limit our view of God's ways to those that we have charted, we will miss any revelation of God that might unfold in what is unexpected. The experience of Elijah should stand as an example for us.

We sometimes trivialize the gospel story, demonstrating a subtle sense of superiority as we consider Peter's lack of faith. One would think that after seeing Jesus perform the miracle of the loaves, Peter would have trusted Jesus' power to support him across the waters. We certainly would have acted more in keeping with our faith. But then, it is one thing to observe divine power at work in the lives of others, and quite another to step out bravely into chaos, confident that that same power will sustain us.

Would that we were like Peter. His faith may not have been strong at all times, but he did show trust in Jesus. This is evident in two ways. When Jesus told him to "come" to him across the raging waters, Peter responded with alacrity; and when the waters began to consume him, he cried to Jesus for the help he presumed he would find in him. It does not seem to have been his lack of faith in Jesus that caused him to sink, but the fury of the waters and the terror that it engendered in him. After all, as a man who fished that lake, Peter would have known better than others the treachery of its waters. Peter did have faith, but it was not enough to overcome his fear.

Who of us has not been in a similar situation? We are initially sincere in our commitment to goodness and integrity, but then the rug is pulled out from under us, or our lives are turned upside down, or someone we love is snatched from our embrace. At such times we can lose faith in God, in each other, and in ourselves. This is not to exonerate Peter, but it is to look honestly at how we all at times deal with life's tragedies. What does God expect of us in such situations? But then, what did Jesus, who is depicted here as wielding the power of the Creator-God, expect of Peter, a simple fisherman?

The second reading presents Paul as passionately in love with Christ, yet willing to be "accursed and cut off from Christ for the sake of my own people, my kindred according to the flesh." His words may be a gross overstatement, but his devotion to his Jewish compatriots is unquestionable. These were and will always continue to be the people chosen by God to bring forth the Christ, according to the flesh. Paul is willing to sacrifice himself for them.

What does God expect of us? No more than has ever been expected of these others: the realization that it is in the very ordinary events of life that we meet God; a willingness to follow Jesus even into the chaos that may overwhelm us; a genuine love for and commitment to others. This is what God expects of us. It is a challenge, but he assures us, "Take courage, it is I; do not be afraid."

Praying with Scripture

- Pray for the grace to be open to the unexpected ways of God.

- Reflect on the lives of people you know who have remained faithful in the midst of great misfortune.

- What sacrifices are you willing to make for the people in your life?

TWENTIETH SUNDAY IN ORDINARY TIME
Readings:
Isa 56:1, 6–7; Ps 67:2–3, 5–6, 8;
Rom 11:13–15, 29–32; Matt 15:21–28

WHO'S IN YOUR CIRCLE?

In the minds of many people, a circle is a symbol of inclusivity. We speak of a circle of family or friends, those who surround us with love and support. In such a configuration, all are equal members. Though there may be obvious differences in age or abilities, there is no real hierarchy of positions. Round tables for discussion are often preferred, for this very reason. All participants can be seen and no one can claim a place of privilege.

Circles can also be very exclusive, however. Their lines define who is included and who is not. Once a circle has been formed, it is very difficult to break it open in order to add more members. In such situations there is often the circle, and then the inner circle. Exclusive circles can be drawn along lines of gender, race, ethnic origin, class, ability, or interest, to name but a few criteria of selection.

One of the great sources of scandal for us is the Christian faith's insistence on the universal embrace of God. At first glance, we might be thrilled with this tenet of our faith. A closer look, however, will show that we are not always happy with the implications of this teaching. An example of this can be found in today's first reading. It speaks of "[t]he foreigners who joined themselves to the LORD…them I will bring to my holy mountain." Doesn't this inclusion of foreigners challenge the privileged position of the "chosen people"? Actually, no!

Though we use the phrase *chosen people* to refer first to the Jewish nation and then to the Christian community, its real meaning is inclusive rather than exclusive. Ancient Israel believed that it was chosen to be the instrument through which all other people would be brought to God. There were times when the people were faithful to this call, when they believed that "all nations shall stream toward [the mountain of the LORD's house]" (Isa 2:2–3; Mic 4:1–2). When they were not faithful, God made sure that those who were considered "outsiders" gained access. In today's Isaian passage, God declares: "…them I will bring to my holy mountain."

In the Gospel we find Jesus forced to step out of any Jewish ethnic bias in order to respond to the persistent pleas of a devoted Canaanite mother. This is a bold parent. Women did not normally speak to men in public, not even to their own husbands. Furthermore, she was a Canaanite woman. It may be true that Jesus was out of the confines of Jewish territory, but the hostility between the two ethnic groups endured on both sides of the territorial boundaries. The woman's maternal concern and her belief in Jesus' power bypassed all prejudice on her part as she defied custom and pleaded her cause. Her concern and her faith carried him beyond such barriers as well, for he was moved to grant her request. His words to her sound harsh to contemporary ears. They reflect the disdain with which the Jewish community sometimes viewed those who were not members of their circle. His compassion showed that neither Jesus himself nor the power of God that he exercised was confined to that circle.

Paul walks a narrow tightrope in today's reading. Throughout his ministry, he insisted that only faith in Jesus could save, not obedience to the laws and customs of Israel. In a sense he has broken through one exclusive circle, only to trace a new one. Here, however, he argues that those with this faith in Jesus are really no better than the Jewish people who did not have it. Paul insists that the Jews have not really been excluded, "for the gifts and the call of God are irrevocable." In fact, all have in one way or another been disobedient. Despite this, all have the mercy of God available to them, because the embrace of God is not a closed circle.

From the very beginning, the church has struggled with the dilemma created by its insistence on faith as a requisite for salvation and its belief in God's loving concern for all people. Down through the ages, various resolutions to the dilemma have been offered. However, the struggle has made its way to us still unresolved in our own day. Despite the variety of solutions given, one point in the argument has stood firm: The embrace of God is not a closed circle.

We live at a time when some insist that if you don't hold the same values that they do, you are not a true believer. Sometimes the accusation is even worse; they maintain that you actually threaten religious values. This disparity in esteeming the religious values of others not only exists between diverse religious cultures, but is found within religious denominations themselves This attitude is contrary to the depiction of authentic biblical faith as found in today's readings.

Praying with Scripture

- Make an effort to invite someone new into your social circle.

- What do you know about other prominent world religions? What might you do about this?

- Pray today's responsorial psalm with a religious or cultural group other than your own in mind.

TWENTY-FIRST SUNDAY IN ORDINARY TIME
Readings:
*Isa 22:19–23; Ps 138:1–3, 6, 8;
Rom 11:33–36; Matt 16:13–20*

SERVANT OF THE PEOPLE OF GOD

It is the middle of the summer. Most people are thinking about relaxing vacations, yet the readings would have us look at leadership, a topic that is anything but relaxing. Isaiah reports on the transfer of leadership, while Matthew recounts the initial bestowal of it. It is clear that Jesus is talking about religious leadership; at first glance, one might think that Isaiah is referring only to the political realm. However, those in office in ancient Israel had both political and religious responsibilities, and so we can say that both readings today address the issue of religious leadership.

Religious leadership is a sacred trust, not to be assumed by oneself, but accepted as a responsibility conferred by God. Both ancient Israel and early Christianity insisted on this. Today's readings indicate that religious leaders are taken from among the people, appointed by God for the sake of the people, and are accountable to God for the religious well-being of the people. Shebna was in charge of the royal household during the reign of King Hezekiah. Because he did not faithfully fulfill his charge, he was relieved of his responsibilities, which were then given to Eliakim. Meanwhile Shebna was demoted to a much lower office in the monarchy.

One might wonder why Jesus appointed Peter to be the head of his church. Anyone who has read this Gospel will have to admit that Peter never really distinguished himself as a religious leader. As unbelievable as it may have seemed, Peter became the rock upon which the church would be built. However, Jesus did declare, "**I** will build **my** church." It was not to be Peter's church; it was and is Jesus' church, and though being the head of that church certainly has been regarded as a position of honor, as stated earlier, religious leadership of the people of God is primarily a sacred trust. The sacredness of this trust is found not primarily in the leadership itself, but in the church, because the people are a sacred people. The biblical tradition maintains that good religious leaders are really servants of the people. They take their positions and responsibilities seriously, because the people of God deserve the best that they have to offer.

The symbolism in these readings may be unfamiliar to us, but this is no reason for their meaning to be lost. In the first reading, the robe and the sash indicate that Eliakim has been invested with authority. In many instances, distinctive garb is still a sign of special authority. This can be seen in the respect given to judicial robes or academic garb. The key symbolizes jurisdiction, and the tent peg is a sign of stability. The gospel reading includes no account of investiture, but we do find other symbolism there. Stability is expressed by the familiar play on words that is lost in translation: Peter (*Petros*) is the rock (*petra*) upon which Jesus builds the church. Peter is also endowed with the power of the keys. However, Peter's responsibility here is not principally managerial, as was Eliakim's. Rather, it is juridical. The reading tells us that Peter had a special role in interpreting the law for the rest of the community. At this time in Israel, this was the responsibility of the scribes. In Jesus' church, the task of interpreting the law is entrusted to a simple fisherman.

Paul was very conscious of the unpredictable way in which God chose religious leaders, for he himself had first persecuted the very gospel that he now preached. In today's reading from the Letter to the Romans, he marveled at the inexplicable ways of God who time and again stepped into human lives in unusual ways with saving grace. It was God who initiated and shaped the believing communities depicted in today's readings, and it was God who called some to lead these believing people. Leadership, for Paul, was certainly a sacred trust, not to be taken lightly, either by those who led or by those who were led.

The scandal of unprincipled religious leaders is not simply their flawed nature. Most deplorable is their betrayal of the sacred trust accorded them by God. Theirs is neither an office to cling to as one's right, nor a privileged position that places one above the rest of the people of God. It is a responsibility and to that extent it is a burden, not unlike the heavy key placed on the shoulder of the master of the royal household. Furthermore, it is a responsibility that can be taken away as quickly and efficiently as it was given, as the story about Shebna shows. Those who have been called to religious leadership would do well to keep the final words of today's responsorial psalm in mind:

> The LORD is exalted, yet the lowly he sees,
> and the proud he knows from afar.

Praying with Scripture

- What is your attitude toward leadership of any kind?

- Is your own leadership characterized by control of the situation or by service of others?

- Pray that religious leaders will be faithful to their sacred trust.

TWENTY-SECOND SUNDAY IN ORDINARY TIME
Readings:
Jer 20:7–9; Ps 63:2–6, 8–9;
Rom 12:1–2; Matt 16:21–27

THE PRICE OF FIDELITY

Nobody wants to suffer! Every living being cringes from pain. It is almost as if we have within us a driving force to run away from it. And then we come across readings like today's that admonish us "to offer [our] bodies as a living sacrifice." They seem to call us to act against our very nature. In the past, they bolstered a spirituality that claimed that the more severe the physical deprivation the greater would be the spiritual benefits. In the recent past, we have come to realize that such notions fail to grasp the goodness of our corporeality, and they misunderstand the biblical injunction that we find in today's passage from the Letter to the Romans. A closer reading will show that today's readings really exhort us to respond joyfully to God's invitation to intimacy regardless of the cost, and not simply to embrace suffering in itself.

The touching depiction of Jeremiah makes this distinction clear. He did not want to be a prophet in the first place (Jer 1:6). He finally did acquiesce, only to find that his words, which were really God's words, were not heeded. More than that, he was forced to suffer because of the responsibility placed on him by God. The personal derision and humiliation that he endured prompted him to resolve never again to proclaim God's message to his compatriots. However, the word of God within him would not be stilled. Like a burning fire in the depths of his being, it flared out despite his resolve never again to speak.

Jeremiah did not seek suffering; in fact, he seems to have done whatever he could to avoid it. But it was the price he was forced to pay for being faithful to his mission. He suffered because his own people were hard-hearted and refused to accept God's message. It seems that he would suffer regardless of the decision he made about his ministry. Fidelity to his call met with persecution; resistance to it resulted in interior affliction.

In the Gospel, the disciples are called to follow Jesus. Like others who came to see him, they were inflamed by his words and captivated by his miraculous powers. In today's reading, Jesus shows them the other side of what it means to be a disciple: "Deny yourself; take up your cross and follow me." As was the case with the first reading, the issue here is fidelity to one's call, not suffering in itself. The disciples are told that if they want to follow Jesus, they must be willing to accept the same kind of rejection that he was enduring and to pay the price that he was willing to pay.

Peter's misplaced enthusiastic support of Jesus shows that he had not understood this. His reaction was so like our own might be. He might have told Jesus, "Cut your losses and run!" The response that his advice provoked shows Jesus' firm commitment to his mission. No obstacle will deter him, not even the sincere yet misguided concern of his close friends.

The focus of these two readings helps us better understand Paul's admonishment "to offer your bodies as a living sacrifice." He was no more advocating suffering for its own sake than Jeremiah or Jesus had. Rather, Paul realized that suffering or sacrifice might be required of those who respond faithfully to their call to be disciples. Paul was quite explicit in identifying the real cause of suffering: "Do not conform yourselves to this age but be transformed by the renewal of your mind." He admonished the early Christians to turn away from those social practices that were opposed to gospel values and to live disciplined lives. He knew from his own experience both the anger this could engender in others and the inner struggle that personal reform could produce. He instructed the Christians, "[O]ffer your bodies as a living sacrifice."

The suffering discussed in these readings should not surprise us because we know that sacrifice is often the price we pay for fidelity to our calling in life. Parents exhibit this in their willingness to give their lives for their children. Anyone who works to improve society must harbor deep convictions in order to face what often appear to be insurmountable obstacles. This is true about any kind of genuine commitment. The commitment itself can make tremendous demands on us. One's calling does not always come from the outside. Sometimes God places a desire to help others that burns from deep within one's heart. As we strive to respond faithfully to our calling, whatever that calling may be, Paul's words can take on profound meaning: "Be transformed by the renewal of your mind, that you may discern what is the will of God, what is good and pleasing and perfect."

Praying with Scripture

- In what ways have you responded to God's call in your life?

- What has this call cost you?

- Pray that you may be willing and able to pay the price that fidelity might exact of you.

TWENTY-THIRD SUNDAY IN ORDINARY TIME
Readings:
Ezek 33:7–9; Ps 95:1–2, 6–9; Rom 13:8–10; Matt 18:15–20

IT'S NONE OF MY BUSINESS!

We all know individuals who pride themselves on "keeping their noses out of other people's business." There certainly is no virtue in being a busybody, but neither is disregard for others something about which we should boast. We often promote attitudes of self-reliance and independence, attitudes to be praised. However, these attitudes may really be unabashed self-centeredness and radical individualism. Many believe that, if no one is getting hurt, the interests and concerns of others are none of my business, and mine are none of theirs.

On the other hand, some societies are so group oriented that the value of the individual almost seems to be lost. Personal preferences are regularly sacrificed for what is considered the common good. Unique talents or interests are renounced as threats to the status quo. There is no privacy; there are no secrets. One's value is derived from one's usefulness. Such extreme points of view benefit neither the group nor the individual. We may be social beings, but we are also unique creations of God, each possessing an innate drive to unfold in surprising new ways. We need the community to thrive, and the community needs each of us to develop. The challenge is to hold these two aspects in balance.

Ezekiel is told that he will be a "watchman for the house of Israel." He is answerable to God for the spiritual well-being of others. As spokesperson of God, he must convey God's word to the people, but it will be their responsibility to accept that word and to follow its direction. Anyone who has ever had to "lay down the law" knows that this can be not only a thankless task, but also often one that exacts a dear price. If only Ezekiel had simply minded his own business! As "watchman of the house of Israel," however, the spiritual well-being of the community *was* his business. Here we see the intimate relationship between the righteousness of one member and the religious soundness of the entire group. The character of the group consists largely of the combined character of its members.

In the gospel reading Jesus insists that it is not enough for Christians to "mind their own business." Each is responsible for the spiritual well-being of the entire community. Here the community suffers from the sinfulness of one of its members. Reconciliation between the sinner and the one sinned against is necessary for the spiritual health of the entire group. Note that it is the aggrieved member who initiates the reconciliation. In other words, forgiveness precedes communal healing.

The steps to be followed in this process of reconciliation are significant. First, address the offense where it occurred, between the individuals concerned. If this fails, bring a few others into the process. Only if this fails should it become a public matter. If we think of the believing community as a family rather than as a corporate organization, we can appreciate the relationship between an individual and the entire group. The goodness and the failings of one member affect the entire family; all can feel the alienation of some.

It is difficult to assume responsibility for the entire community, especially today. The local parish can be so large that it is impossible to know many of the members. Furthermore, some people treat the church like a kind of spiritual supermarket. They stop in to get what they need, they make the appropriate monetary contribution, and they only return when they need something again. Nor do people always go to the neighborhood church anymore. They often shop around for the best product. The parish church is no longer the principal gathering place where parishioners are neighbors and children play together.

This change in the character of church community does not absolve us of our communal responsibilities; it merely poses new challenges. We continue to be responsible for the spiritual well-being of the church. As difficult as it may be, we are still obliged to warn others of the pitfalls of contemporary life. We can do this through the way we raise our children, through the way we conduct business or participate in political life. The individual does make a difference.

Perhaps one of the most difficult challenges before us today lies in the realm of reconciliation. We live in a world of overwhelming turmoil. Parents and children, sisters and brothers are alienated; there is tremendous animosity within the church; governments no longer enjoy the trust and respect of their citizens; nations continue to nurse centuries-old grudges; and terrorism threatens us all. We will never experience real peace until we are willing to admit our faults and/or initiate the very difficult process of reconciliation. As we take even faltering steps toward such reconciliation, however, we are assured that Jesus will be in our midst.

Praying with Scripture

- Prayerfully read today's psalm response. To what might God be calling you?

- What kind of influence are you in the life of another?

- With whom must you be reconciled? What steps can you take to realize this?

TWENTY-FOURTH SUNDAY IN ORDINARY TIME

Readings:
Sir 27:30—28:9; Ps 103:1–4, 9–12;
Rom 14:7–9; Matt 18:21–35

"HOW OFTEN MUST I FORGIVE?"

Last week's readings spoke of reconciliation. This week we consider the same theme, but from the perspective of forgiveness. We all know how hard it is to say that we are sorry when we have offended another; but it may be even harder to forgive when we have been offended. And yet, we pledge to do this every time we say the Lord's Prayer: "Forgive us our trespasses, as we forgive those who trespass against us." We know this prayer so well that we might not realize the challenge to which we commit ourselves each time we pray it.

Some say that a feature unique to the Christian religion is its insistence on forgiveness. Today's reading from Sirach shows that this is not quite the case. Jesus' admonition to forgive came right out of his own Jewish tradition. Sirach instructs the Jewish people of his day: "Forgive your neighbor's injustice; then when you pray, your own sins will be forgiven." Sirach knew that wrath and vengeance can erode the spirit of the one who harbors such attitudes, and that forgiveness and mercy have the power to heal not only the offender but the one offended as well. He also questioned the virtue of one who asked for mercy and forgiveness, but who refused to grant it to others. It seems as if Jesus' teaching on forgiveness came right out of the Book of Sirach.

What is unique, however, is Jesus' insistence on continual forgiveness. Peter asked, "How often must I forgive? As many as seven times?" Since the common teaching of the time required that one forgive an offender at least three times, Peter must have thought that seven times, a number that implied completeness, would have been a magnanimous gesture. Jesus startles him with his response: "I say to you, not seven times but seventy-seven times." In other words, there is no limit to the number of times we must be willing to forgive. Now *this* is the scandal of Christian forgiveness. This does not mean that we must "forgive and forget." No, we must not forget, but not so that we cannot exact vengeance. Rather, we must not forget so that the offense will not be repeated.

Both readings tell us why we should forgive. Sirach says it is because we too are "but flesh," weak human beings who also seek God's forgiveness. Jesus gives the same reason, and then he tells a story to emphasize that what God has forgiven us far outstrips what we are asked to forgive.

This teaching on forgiveness flies in the face of much of today's thinking. Some people continue to carry resentment toward someone from their childhood, perhaps their parents. Rather than do what we can to resolve petty differences, we take them to court. Traffic misunderstandings often result in violent road rage. What has happened to us? We do not easily forgive the human weaknesses of others. Yet this is precisely what we are called to do. This is not to say that we should put aside justice. Society requires order and the sanctions that seek to ensure it. However, so many offenses are really due to oversight, not "malice of intent."

Still, how does one forgive a pedophile whose behavior robs children of their innocence and undermines their chances for healthy intimacy? How does one forgive a murderer who has snuffed out the life of a loved one? And will the world ever be able to forgive terrorists who blow up innocent people? On occasion we do hear of heroic individuals who, by the grace of God, have been able to move beyond hatred and vengeance to embrace genuine forgiveness. Recently, several members of an Amish community attended the funeral of a man who committed suicide after he had executed several Amish children in their schoolhouse. Committed to peace and nonviolence, these heroic and generous people sought to console the family of that murderer. Such heroes do exist. Most of us, however, cannot claim to be among their number.

Is this exhortation to forgive pointless because it seems to be impossible to achieve? Perhaps for many of us it is an ideal toward which we strive. If we cannot yet forgive, at least we must rid our hearts of vengeance, for it will do more harm to us than to those whom we hate. If we cannot yet forgive crimes that have been perpetrated against us, we certainly can make every effort to forgive the petty mistakes of others. We can learn to makes amends when impatience flares up, or frustration overwhelms us or others. We will hardly be able to forgive serious offenses if we cannot overlook slights. The more we can learn to forgive others, the more we will become like God who so generously forgives us, "not seven times but seventy-seven times."

Praying with Scripture

- How generously are you involved in the lives of others?

- With whom must you be reconciled? What steps can you take to realize this?

- Pray for the grace to cleanse your mind and heart of all traces of vengeance.

TWENTY-FIFTH SUNDAY IN ORDINARY TIME
Readings:
Isa 55:6–9; Ps 145:2–3, 8–9, 17–18; Phil 1:20c–24, 27a; Matt 20:1–16a

IS OUR GENEROUS GOD FAIR?

I sometimes think that the parables enjoy a popularity that may be misplaced. I do not question their extraordinary composition or their radical religious message; it is just that we may be identifying with the wrong person in the story and then missing the really subversive flavor of the story. The parable in today's Gospel dispels any doubt about the challenge always placed before us by these remarkable accounts.

We might find this parable disturbing because we identify ourselves with those "who bore the day's burden and the heat." I am sure we want God to be generous, but sometimes we might expect that God's generosity be proportionate to the duration and quality of one's commitment. This parable shows that the criterion by which God operates is not the standard that most of us might follow. According to human standards, our generous God does not seem to be fair. We have learned that God is all-knowing, all-loving, all-just, all-everything-that-is-good. Therefore, we are afraid to suggest that God might not be fair. We are afraid that such a statement could be a kind of blasphemy. But then, how is this parable to be understood?

Perhaps we should understand it as a concrete example of what is found in the last lines of today's reading from the prophet Isaiah:

> For my thoughts are not your thoughts,
> nor are your ways my ways, says the LORD.
> As high as the heavens are above the earth,
> so high are my ways above your ways
> and my thoughts above your thoughts.

The prophet very clearly states that we simply cannot understand God or the ways of God. In fact, even our best theological statements can lead to misunderstanding. This limitation calls to mind the negative way of speaking of God developed in the theology of the Eastern Church. Called apophatic, it explicitly acknowledges the inadequacy of the human mind to grasp the things of God. Does this then strip the parables of their religious value? Certainly not! But it does remind us that even the parables of Jesus can provide only glimpses of the ways of God. And even when they do accomplish this, if taken too literally, they might very well misrepresent another aspect of the divine reality. After all, parables are merely human compositions.

What, then, is the point of today's parable? It clearly states that God calls people at different times during their lifetimes. We know from experience that this is a fact, and so we can accept it as true. The parable also says that those who respond positively to this call from God are promised "what is just." Again, this flows from an understanding of God that we have come to know, and so we can accept it as well. However, then the parable turns our understanding of fairness upside down. But this is what makes it so powerful! It appears to tell us something about God, when in fact it may be revealing our own arrogance and selfishness.

Perhaps we understand the story from the wrong perspective. If we identify with those "who bore the day's burden and the heat," in other words, those who deserve "what is just," we may be troubled by God's generosity. We might even be tempted to judge this generosity as being unfair. If we identify with the undeserving ones, however, those who may even be an afterthought, we will be thrilled with divine generosity. What, after all, makes us identify with those we consider deserving and not with those who are the latecomers?

Divine generosity is always a scandal to people who believe that it should only be granted to those who deserve it. And it is in this conviction that their error is laid bare, for no one deserves the generosity of God. It is a free gift, given to all who will accept it. If we think we deserve it, we will resent those who in our judgment do not. It is arrogant to think that we have earned God's blessings; it is selfish to want to hug them to ourselves.

In today's short passage from Philippians, Paul displays remarkable unselfishness toward others. He was certainly one "who bore the day's burden and the heat." Yet, for the sake of others, he was willing to remain working in the vineyard. He knew the generosity of God, and he decided to continue to act as an agent of that generosity as long as he was able.

The reign of God is a reign of divine generosity. We are invited to participate in it. If God invites others, we should be happy that they join us. Divine generosity is not a limited commodity. The enjoyment of others will take nothing from ours. On the contrary, if we truly share in the generosity of God, their enjoyment will enhance ours.

Praying with Scripture

- In what ways might you be trying to limit the ways of God?

- Can you genuinely rejoice in the good fortune of others?

- Pray for an open and generous heart.

TWENTY-SIXTH SUNDAY IN ORDINARY TIME
Readings:
Ezek 18:25–28; Ps 25:4–9;
Phil 2:1–11; Matt 21:28–32

DON'T YOU KNOW WHO I AM?

The passage from Philippians read today captures the very essence of both the incarnation and our redemption through Jesus Christ. Often referred to as the "Christ Hymn," it includes an exhortation to fashion our own minds and hearts after Jesus' example of humble self-sacrifice. Paul states that "though [Jesus] was in the form of God [he] did not regard equality with God something to be grasped." In poetic fashion, Paul here explains the incarnation as a kind of relinquishing of divine privilege. He does not say that Jesus renounced his divine character, but that he set it aside and assumed instead the form of a servant or slave.

This picture of a humble Jesus is confirmed by various gospel accounts. Nowhere do we find him demanding, or even expecting, that others accord him the respect that was his due. There is no condescending query, "Don't you know who I am?" On the contrary, he made himself available to others, meeting their needs, supporting them in their efforts. Jesus not only stepped down from the exalted heights of divinity, but he also refrained from claiming any kind of human entitlement. Instead, he chose to be the servant of all. The humility evident in the incarnation is placed before us today for our imitation.

The extent of Jesus' sacrifice of himself for others is seen in his self-immolation for our redemption. "He humbled himself, becoming obedient to the point of death." If in the incarnation he set aside his divine privilege in order to show us how to be truly human, by his death for our redemption he showed us how to be willing to pay the price that may be exacted when we are faithful to our calling as Christians. By dying for us as he did, he relinquished even the human dignity that was his. Jesus truly emptied himself for our sake.

Paul's exhortation is startling: "Do nothing out of selfishness or out of vainglory." This was a demanding challenge to a society governed by principles of honor and shame. One's place in such a society was determined by one's reputation. (Don't you know who I am?) To suggest that one humble oneself was unthinkable. Yet this is precisely what Paul was urging, and he offered the image of the humble Jesus as a model to follow.

The tension between honor and shame plays an important role in the gospel reading as well. There, however, these principles are turned upside down. The "chief priests and elders of the people" were the respected leaders of the community. They were responsible to see that societal standards were upheld. To this end, they often passed judgment on the behavior of others. This was why Jesus told the story he did.

In the story, the actions of both sons offended their father. The first son's "no" was a public insult; it shamed his father. However, he had a change of heart and he then fulfilled his father's request. The second son was not guilty of public affront, but neither did he accede to his father's wishes. The first son was a repentant public sinner; the second son appeared to be faithful, but was not.

After the leaders judged in favor of the first son, Jesus placed their decision at their own doorstep. Though not public sinners, they were nonetheless unacceptable. Tax collectors were despised because they collaborated with the occupying Roman government. Prostitutes were denounced because they disregarded the mores of the patriarchal society. However, Jesus proclaims that these dishonorable people were more acceptable than the respected leaders. Why? Might it be because of the arrogance of these leaders? They stood in judgment over others, presuming that their own observance of the law made them righteous. What right had Jesus to accuse them? Didn't he know who they were?

Just what does make one acceptable? Clearly it is not status, for Paul insists that, following the example of Jesus, we must be willing to set aside any privilege that might be ours. Nor is it public acceptance, for Jesus tells us that even social honor can be deceiving. Then what is it? Paul maintains that it is humility and service of others; Jesus contends that it is faith and repentance.

No one of us is in a position to assume the moral high ground and, looking down on others, to challenge them with "Don't you know who I am?" We are all weak, limited human beings, who time and again have strayed from the path of righteousness and who are in need of God's mercy and forgiveness. As we see in the first reading, God's mercy and forgiveness will be granted us if we repent of our waywardness. The psalm response highlights this same theme: "In your kindness remember me." We can be certain of this forgiveness, for the psalm also states that God "guides the humble to justice."

Praying with Scripture

- In which specific area of your life must you set aside privilege for the sake of others?

- Whom do you hold in high esteem, and why?

- Make the responsorial psalm your prayer today.

TWENTY-SEVENTH SUNDAY IN ORDINARY TIME
Readings:
Isa 5:1–7; Ps 80:9, 12–16, 19–20; Phil 4:6–9; Matt 21:33–43

DIVINE TLC

There is something exotic about a vineyard. But then I am from the Midwest, where the landscape is dotted with dairy farms. And I am a city girl, who never experienced the rigors or disappointments associated with cultivating a crop. (I do remember that, like many others, my grandfather made wine in the cellar, which was hardly exotic!) I am sure that my fascination with viticulture can be traced back to the Bible stories of my early childhood. I concluded that any land that produced figs, dates, and wine must have been wondrous.

In painting pictures of vineyards, today's readings lead us through the development of two themes: God's tender loving care and the undependability of those entrusted with the vineyard. Like good theologians, the biblical writers used what they knew from experience as metaphors for telling us something about God and God's dealings with us. This is clearly seen in the reading from Isaiah. The picture sketched there by the prophet is both sensitive and disheartening. The vineyard was carefully planted and cared for, yet it did not produce a crop of luscious, sweet-tasting grapes; instead, it brought forth wild grapes.

Though the prophet states, "My friend had a vineyard," it is clear that God is really the vinedresser. The details of the metaphor emphasize the great effort put forth into preparing the kind of soil necessary to ensure a rich and abundant yield. Spading and clearing away stones, done by hand in ancient Israel, demonstrate God's painstaking commitment to this future vineyard. When the preparatory work was completed and the tender young vines were placed in the soil, the vinedresser constructed a watchtower meant to provide protection against possible predatory animals and unscrupulous poachers. What are we to make of God's tender loving care?

The psalm reinforces this description of God's providential care. While the prophet focused on the land that would become the vineyard, the psalmist speaks about the vine itself. It was transplanted from Egypt. God uprooted it from foreign soil where it could not thrive, solicitously carried it across the desert, and then carefully planted it in the soil that had been meticulously prepared. Here too we see that, despite God's tender loving care, the walls meant to protect the vineyard were breached and the precious vineyard was violated. One gets the sense that, as was the case in the passage from Isaiah, the vineyard was responsible for its own devastation.

The attentiveness of the landowner in the Gospel corresponds with the description of the vinedresser found in Isaiah. However, the parable focuses on those to whom the vineyard was entrusted rather than on land preparation or the vine that was planted. The unscrupulous tenants plotted to appropriate both the grape harvest and the vineyard itself. What made them think that killing the heir would entitle them to the land? There seems to have been a law in Israel that in the absence of the owner, those who were able to secure immediate possession could claim property. The tenants were well positioned to make this move.

In none of these passages is God an absentee landlord, unconcerned with the vineyard. The passage from Isaiah plainly testifies to God's disappointment and ultimate dismantling of the once-cherished land. The psalm also states that it was God who broke down the walls, allowing every passerby to pluck the fruit and letting animals overrun the vineyard. Divine anger is most clearly depicted in the gospel parable. This may be due to the treachery that is explicitly outlined.

What is the message here? In the first reading and the psalm response, the vineyard is the house of Israel. In the Gospel it is identified as the reign of God. In each instance, God goes to great lengths to prepare a wondrous blessing. However, those who should have enjoyed this blessing defy God's plan, and so God responds angrily. Only the first reading ends on a note of outrage and punishment. The psalm includes a plea for salvation and new life, and the Gospel states that God's blessings will endure, even if bestowed on other people. We too have been invited into this vineyard, this reign of God. However, we must remember that it really belongs to God; we are but tenants on the land, with obligations to the landowner. Paul lays out some of these obligations. He tells us to commit ourselves to "whatever is true…honorable…just…pure…holy…[and] gracious."

In inviting us to enjoy the riches of this vineyard, God has shown us tender loving care that is unfathomable. All God asks in return is faithfulness, not simply obedience to impersonal laws. God seeks the kind of faithfulness that wells up in us when we know that we are loved and cherished and cared for; the kind of faithfulness that responds wholeheartedly to God's love.

Praying with Scripture

- Think of how you have experienced God's tender loving care in your life.

- In what ways have you disregarded the blessings you have received?

- How are you being called to labor in God's vineyard?

TWENTY-EIGHTH SUNDAY IN ORDINARY TIME
Readings:
*Isa 25:6–10a; Ps 23:1–6;
Phil 4:12–14, 19–20; Matt 22:1–14*

"Food! Glorious Food!"

A scene in *Oliver*, the musical based on Charles Dickens's classic tale *Oliver Twist*, depicts a crowd of ragged, starving urchins celebrating the pleasures of eating: "Food! Glorious food!" Deprived as they were, they certainly appreciated the delight of food, perhaps better than many Americans today. We seem to have an epidemic of obesity, and yet incidents of anorexia and bulimia continue to increase. While many children go to bed hungry, we spend millions of dollars on diet aids and exercise equipment. Eating, one of the most basic functions of every living being, has become a disorder for many people.

If we fail to appreciate the basic function of food, we will certainly not be able to grasp the depth of its potential as a theological metaphor. This is unfortunate, because the readings for today, as well as the psalm response, refer to food.

Breaking bread with another has always been considered a sign of friendship and intimacy. This is particularly true when we eat from a common plate. We take in the same food and somehow we are bonded with each other. Eating together also signifies trust, because during a meal we lower our guard. Finally, in many societies, the hospitality extended by the host and accepted by the guest establishes reconciliation between possible enemies, if only for the duration of the meal. Much of this profound meaning has been lost in today's fast-food culture.

As we approach the end of the liturgical year, the Sunday readings begin to touch on "end-time" themes. Though they are often closely associated, "end-time" is not the same as "end of time," a concept so very popular with many evangelical groups today. In the Bible, the end-time is the time of fulfillment of God's promises. Ancient Israel thought of this time as the messianic age. Jesus spoke of this age as the reign of God. It might find its completion at the end of time, but the coming of Jesus into history inaugurated that age in the here and now. We Christians believe that we now live in the reign of God, in the messianic age, in the end-time.

What can compare with sharing a fabulous meal of scrumptious food and delightful drink, surrounded by those we love? Is it any wonder that this is the way we celebrate birthdays, weddings, and anniversaries? Is it any wonder that this would be a favorite metaphor for characterizing the end-time? This is precisely what the readings do today.

Isaiah paints a picture of "a feast of rich food and choice wines." It is a picture of the end-time, the time in which we live. It is the time when God brings all people together to enjoy the same meal. Sharing that meal turns enemies into friends and kindred. The prophet paints a very touching scene of reconciliation with God and with all others, and this is celebrated with a banquet.

The psalm response reminds us who the host of this banquet really is. Employing what may be the best-known biblical metaphor, the psalmist describes how, like a totally committed shepherd, God spares nothing to provide nourishment for the flock. Only the barest outlines of the meal are provided. However, the peacefulness of the setting is undeniable: "in verdant pastures...beside restful waters...you spread the table before me." This is certainly a picture of fulfillment.

The gospel parable of the wedding feast is rich in end-time imagery. Jesus himself characterizes the reign of God as a wedding feast, a banquet of "calves and fatted cattle." Here the powerful end-time themes of decision and judgment are introduced. Many have been invited to the banquet, but they do not accept the invitation. Have they forgotten that celebratory meals mean more than simply eating and drinking? Have they turned their backs on friendship and intimacy, trust and reconciliation? It appears so. However, the wedding has taken place and the banquet honoring that union has been prepared. There is going to be a celebration! The king is intent on it!

The parable may have been directed originally toward those who opposed Jesus. If they would not accept him as Messiah, they certainly would refuse an invitation to a messianic banquet in his honor. Though the parable condemns them for their obstinacy, it also challenges us. Have we accepted God's invitation to the messianic banquet? Have we even recognized or understood the invitation? Banqueting implies friendship and intimacy, trust and reconciliation. Are these attitudes integral components of our lives?

Though it is relatively easy to accept an invitation to a banquet, it is vastly more difficult to develop an end-time point of view in which we celebrate intimacy and reconciliation. Paul, who was probably in prison when he wrote the Letter to the Philippians, tells us, "I can do all things in him who strengthens me." And so can we.

Praying with Scripture

- Strengthen the bond of love and friendship with someone by sharing a meal.

- Pray for the grace to be reconciled with someone from whom you might be alienated.

- Make the psalm response your prayer today.

TWENTY-NINTH SUNDAY IN ORDINARY TIME
Readings:
Isa 45:1, 4–6; Ps 96:1, 3–5, 7–10; 1 Thess 1:1–5b; Matt 22:15–21

How Does God Work?

The gospels often depict Jesus in conflict with those who are in positions of leadership, both religious and political. A close look will show that Jesus does not challenge legitimate authority, but only the way individuals exercise it. In an upcoming episode, he counsels those around him to heed the scribes and the Pharisees, because they occupy "the chair of Moses" (Matt 23:2). Today he directs them, and us, to fulfill lawful civic duties.

Both the first reading and the gospel passage for today allude to the very difficult political realities of the times. In the two instances, the people were forced to live under foreign domination. The Persian king Cyrus ruled the early Israelites; the Romans occupied the land of the Jews at the time of Jesus. We should remember that the Israelites took great pride in being the nation that God had liberated from foreign rule. Their very identity was synonymous with freedom. But here they are, captive and subject to nonbelievers. The biblical writers do not speak against the captors. On the contrary, both Cyrus and Caesar seem to have a role in God's plan for God's people.

Isaiah refers to Cyrus as the anointed of the LORD, a title usually ascribed to the Davidic king. Furthermore, God grasps the right hand of this Persian king, a gesture that signifies the conferral of royal authority. In other words, Cyrus exercises legitimate authority over the people of God, despite the fact that he is a nonbeliever. God works through this king, and God's plans unfold through him even though he is unaware of it. It was Cyrus who issued the decree that all captured peoples should be allowed to return to their own lands and there take up their lives once again, though still subject to the jurisdiction of the Persian Empire. Thus the people of God left Babylon, the land of their exile, and returned to Israel.

The gospel story is a bit more complicated than it might appear. The self-righteous scribes and Pharisees try to entrap Jesus: "Is it lawful to pay the census tax to Caesar or not?" That is, should we recognize the authority of this nonbeliever? If Jesus answers no, he appears to be politically insubordinate. If he answers yes, he denies Israel's boast of being a people freed from all loyalties other than those that bound them to God.

Jesus turns their entrapment against them by asking for a coin appropriate for paying the census tax. They expose their own complicity with the ruling powers by producing a Roman coin. Such coins did not comply with Israel's prohibition against casting graven images. The scribes and Pharisees are carrying images of the Roman ruler who claimed to be a god. Without either condoning or condemning the character of Roman coins, Jesus instructs them to fulfill lawful civic duties.

In these two accounts we see that fidelity to one's religious tradition, while at the same time granting allegiance to secular powers, is not only possible but is also God's will for us. They show us that, as delicate as the balance between these two very different loyalties might be, they need not be in conflict.

Also prominent in these readings is the theme of insider/outsider. This dynamic was very significant in all of Israel's history and it has taken on great importance in our own day. Many groups are somewhat wary of "outsiders." Those who are not "insiders" could disrupt life; they might even be enemies. This is particularly true of groups that are in any way vulnerable. A threat from an outsider might undermine the little stability that the group enjoys. Both of today's readings come from times when Israel was politically vulnerable, dominated by a stronger nation. It stands to reason that they might not be open to outsiders. Add to this their conviction that they alone were God's chosen people, and we might detect an attitude of religious superiority.

Today's readings challenge the possibility of such an attitude. The people may have viewed Cyrus and Caesar as threats, but God certainly did not. In fact, these men became instruments in God's plan. They may not have believed in the God of Israel, but that did not stop God from using them for good. When it comes to God's plan of salvation, there are no real outsiders. All women and men of goodwill are insiders.

We live in a time when political and religious differences pit us against each other, when persons of another persuasion or faith are considered outsiders or nonbelievers. Whenever we hold such views we fail to see the goodwill of others and we might overlook the good that God is working, for our own benefit, through the agency of those others. We may in fact be making ourselves outsiders to the grace of God active in our world today.

Praying with Scripture

- Do you view those who are not Christian as possible agents of God in your life?

- Find a way to bring an "outsider" into your circle of concern.

- Pray for the grace to recognize God working through legitimate authority, whether religious or civic.

THIRTIETH SUNDAY IN ORDINARY TIME
Readings:
Exod 22:20–26; Ps 18:2–4, 47, 51;
1 Thess 1:5c–10; Matt 22:34–40

"IF WE ONLY HAVE LOVE"

Every once in a while, the world of popular music brings forth a song that can captivate our minds with its beautiful simplicity and lift our yearning souls heavenward. Jacques Brel's "If We Only Have Love" is such a song. The melody is simple enough to grasp after singing only a few bars, but it is the lyrics of the twelve short stanzas that touch us deeply: According to the song, it is love that will open our arms wide to embrace all; it is love that will melt guns so that all the children of the world will be able to live in peace. As seemingly insignificant as human beings might be, with love in our hearts we will be able to accomplish what time, or space, or stars alone cannot accomplish. Some critics might think that the words of this ballad are trite and the melody monotonous. But no one can question the profundity and challenge of the sentiments expressed, sentiments that reflect the message of today's readings.

The law of biblical Israel has often been erroneously characterized as legalistic. Today's passage from Exodus, taken from the section of the book that contains covenant law, paints an entirely different picture. It depicts a nation concerned with its most vulnerable members. We should remember that this was a patriarchal society. In such a society, those with no male patron had little, if any, legal protection. In Israel, three such vulnerable groups were widows, orphans, and aliens. Here they represent all vulnerable people in need of protection.

The reading contains a warning against taking advantage of the less fortunate. God's wrath will flare up against such exploitation; God will hear their prayers and will show them compassion. It is because of such passages that the church's social justice writings of the '60s coined the phrase "preferential option for the poor." This phrase must be understood within the context of the covenant. As covenant partners of God, we have the serious responsibility of caring for the disadvantaged covenant members among us. If we fail to do so, God will side with them. In other words, enjoyment of covenant blessings will be ours "if we only have love."

The gospel account is well known to all. A lawyer, an expert in interpretation of the law, asks Jesus which of the current 613 prohibitions and prescriptions was the greatest. Well versed in his religious tradition, Jesus quotes two passages: "You shall love the Lord your God" (Deut 6:5), and "You shall love your neighbor as yourself" (Lev 19:18). That he knew the law was not remarkable. What is astounding is the way he links these two prescriptions. He places love of neighbor alongside love of God. In fact, he insists that "the whole law and the prophets [the entire religious tradition] depend on these two commandments."

The psalm lists some of the reasons for loving God. God is our strength, our rock, our fortress, our deliverer; God is our shield, the horn of our salvation, our stronghold. God cares for us as no other can care for us, and so we love God. But why should we love our neighbor? What do they do for us? And who is our neighbor? (In Leviticus, "neighbor" refers to other Israelites, other members of the covenant community. Jesus will ultimately expand "neighbor" to include those outside the community as well.) We are to love others, because with them we are in covenant with God, and we show our love for God by the way we love them.

Paul was an example for the Thessalonian Christians of one who loves both God and neighbor. For love of God, he unselfishly poured out his life for those to whom he ministered. Without being specific, he applauds the Thessalonians for imitating him and the Lord as they "became a model for all the believers," presumably in the way they love God and others.

The words of Jacques Brel could be heard as a clarion call to create a new world. This world will be the kind of covenant community depicted in Exodus; it will be the reign of God as proclaimed by Jesus. The world envisioned by these readings is a world in which we warmly embrace the young and the old, rather than exploit them for our own purposes. It is a world in which we bequeath peace and prosperity to the next generation, rather than war and the debt that it incurs. It is a world in which we recognize that, despite our own lowliness, the power of God can work within us to create something marvelous. We will not be limited by the confines of time or space; we will find our place in the vast scope of creation along with the sun and the stars. By the grace of God, we can really accomplish great things, "if we only have love."

Praying with Scripture

- How has being loved by another enriched your life?

- What can you do to alleviate the suffering of someone less fortunate than you?

- In what ways might you "become a model for all the believers"?

THIRTY-FIRST SUNDAY IN ORDINARY TIME
Readings:
*Mal 1:14b—2:2b, 8–10; Ps 131:1–3;
1 Thess 2:7b–9, 13; Matt 23:1–2*

WHO'S RESPONSIBLE HERE?

It was only a few months ago that we reflected on religious leadership (Twenty-first Sunday of Ordinary Time). Today's readings place this theme before us again. The frequency with which the Bible considers religious leadership points out both its importance and its challenge. Because of human weakness, the same abuses of power and authority creep into the exercise of religious leadership as are found in forms of societal or political leadership. The readings for today speak to these abuses.

The memory of the Babylonian exile should have seared the consciousness of the Israelites of the prophet Malachi's day. Initially, the people had interpreted that catastrophe as divine punishment for their repeated infidelities. Time and again, however, they slipped right back into religious laxity. Malachi held the priests of his day largely responsible for the nation's unfaithfulness. Today's first reading does not focus on the priests' cultic duties, but on their role as teachers, for it was the priests who interpreted the law for the people (Deut 17:8–11). According to Malachi the failure of these priests to provide clear and faithful direction for the people actually "caused many to falter."

Though leaders may be blatantly irresponsible, their authority is not thereby illegitimate. Even in such cases, they are to be obeyed. The tragedy is that legitimate authority figures can sometimes be untrustworthy. This is the situation depicted in the gospel account. The scribes and the Pharisees who took "their seat on the chair of Moses" were lawful leaders. The scribes were considered experts in the law, and the Pharisees might be best thought of as "lay theologians." Jesus recognized their authority, and he admonished his followers to do so as well. However, he also cautioned them, "Do and observe all things whatsoever they tell you, but do not follow their example."

Jesus did not accuse the religious leaders of his day of the kind of infidelity of which those at the time of Malachi were guilty. Instead, he opposed the way many of them placed themselves above other people, presuming to be more religious and thriving on the special attention that their office afforded them. They did nothing to lighten the burden placed on those who were needy, nor did they lift even a finger to help them carry it. Their lifestyle was excessive, their appearance was ostentatious, and their appetite for adulation was insatiable. It is no wonder that Jesus directed his followers to avoid imitating them. These were to be humble, as Jesus was humble.

In the psalm response, the psalmist is depicted as humble and unassuming, totally dependent on God "like a weaned child on its mother's lap." This is the kind of leadership that Malachi would have wished for the people of his day, leadership that is humble and dependent on God. It is also the kind of leadership that Jesus wanted for his community.

Paul employed the same metaphor of the nursing mother as he assured the Thessalonian Christians of his tender love for them. He drew on various aspects of maternal devotion as he pointed to aspects of his own ministerial commitment to them. It is unusual for a man from a patriarchal society to use female metaphors to describe his own behavior or his emotional perspective, yet Paul was evidently convinced that such imagery could best capture the essence of his own devotion to his people.

Perhaps these readings are meant more for leaders than for the average believer. They underscore the fact that religious leadership is a sacred responsibility of service to others, not a reward for personal achievement. Jesus insisted that religious leaders should be humble servants of others, not pretentious attention seekers. Paul is a prime example of the humble, devoted leader. Leaders would do well to reflect on his message to the Thessalonians today. Though they do not offer us a clear path to follow, today's readings are meant for us as well. We certainly can recognize inappropriate, even scandalous, behavior in some of our leaders. However, we must be careful that we not then dismiss the legitimate teaching of those leaders. Besides, according to which guidelines do we determine illegitimate teaching? Do we simply accept whatever leaders say, as seems to be indicated in the Gospel? Or, going to the other extreme, does their sinfulness cause us to reject their teaching, as is found in the first reading? Today all of us, not merely our leaders, are responsible for being informed about our faith. Parishes offer many opportunities for learning, and good reading is available to all. Such available ongoing formation does not exonerate religious leaders from their responsibilities. Rather, it demonstrates that believers are mature members of the church and deserve leaders who recognize this and foster their continued growth in the faith.

Praying with Scripture

- Think of a religious leader who has touched your heart. What most impressed you about this person?

- What is the character of the leadership that you exercise?

- Pray today for the leaders of the church, that they may be faithful to their sacred trust.

THIRTY-SECOND SUNDAY IN ORDINARY TIME
Readings:
Wis 2:12–16; Ps 63:2–8;
1 Thess 4:13–18; Matt 25:1–13

IT'S ABOUT TIME!

We are a very impatient people, and the advantages of the electronic age have only exacerbated this. We have fast food, instant replay, and news bytes. We become anxious when we have to stand in line at a checkout counter, and we complain when a homily is more than ten minutes long. I know people who will drive around the block rather than wait for the traffic light to change. We just hate to wait!

As we approach the end of the liturgical year, we are reminded that the unfolding of time is in God's hands. We can neither hurry it nor thwart it. We must be prepared for its fulfillment, however, and we will have to wait for the dawning of this fulfillment. The readings for today call our attention to the character of the fulfillment and the manner of our waiting.

We must first ask, "Just what is being fulfilled?" The answer is "the promises of God." The Bible tells us that God promised the people a secure and prosperous future. The word that encompasses all of these blessings is *peace*. God promised peace, not merely the absence of war, but a life that includes everything people need to be happy and to thrive.

The history of ancient Israel reveals how human selfishness and treachery seemed to impede the fulfillment of this promise. However, not even human sinfulness can foil God's plans, and so the people waited anxiously for the time of fulfillment, which came to be known as the "end-time." The Greeks have a word for this unique time, *kairós*. This is a time that stands by itself, a time that is very different from ongoing, ordinary, unfolding time, or *chrónos*. Wondrous events occur in *kairós*. God's promises are fulfilled. We Christians believe that Jesus inaugurated this time of fulfillment, this *kairós*. However, we still live in the world of ordinary time, in *chrónos*, and that is part of the challenge facing us. We must live in an extraordinary way in this ordinary time that believers understand to be the time of fulfillment.

The Gospel employs the metaphor of a marriage celebration to characterize this wondrous time of fulfillment. The virgins are part of the bridal party, and a large party it is. The point of the parable is the necessity of always being prepared, "for you know neither the day nor the hour." All of the virgins were ready for an immediate arrival of the bridegroom and his company, but only half of them were prepared for the long wait.

The reading from Paul shows that the early Christians, and Paul among them, believed that the ascended Jesus would return during their own lifetime and would take them back to heaven with him. The deaths of some of these believers caused great concern. Had they been unfaithful in some way and, therefore, subject to physical death? Or had they perhaps misunderstood the character of this time of fulfillment? Paul reassured them, and then readjusted his own perception of the end-time. He realized that it would not be just a brief moment, but would last for some time. How long? No one knows either "the day or the time."

Inaugurated by Jesus, this end-time is now seen as stretching into the future. Like the wise virgins, we must always be prepared, having enough oil to last even till midnight if necessary. We cannot presume that oil will be available for purchase when needed. We cannot live as if the end is already upon us; yet we must live as if the end is imminent. How are we to do this?

The mysterious figure of Woman Wisdom is offered as a guide for such thoughtful living. Though the passage read today is not usually associated with the end-time, it does contain several features found in the gospel reading, namely, keeping vigil through the night. We are assured that Wisdom will direct us as we live in this complex time. This Wisdom is much more that practical knowledge or "street smarts." She comes from God and is the "perfection of prudence." To seek Wisdom is to seek God. The reading states, however, that while we might indeed seek her, "She makes her own rounds, seeking" us. Wisdom seeks us. Our role is to be open to her invitation.

The challenge placed before us today need not be overpowering. God has invited us to the celebration of the fulfillment of God's promise of peace. We now live in an in-between time, a time of "already-but-not-yet." We already live in that *kairós* inaugurated by Jesus, but it is not yet completely fulfilled. As we move through time, we must "stay awake," always ready, for we do not know when it will be fulfilled. We are not alone in our waiting. We have, as our loyal companion, the Wisdom that comes from God.

Praying with Scripture

- How prepared are you for the unfolding of God's plan?

- What in your life shows that you are living in the end-time?

- Where do you look for the Wisdom that comes from God?

THIRTY-THIRD SUNDAY IN ORDINARY TIME
Readings:
Prov 31:10–13, 19–20, 30–31; Ps 128:1–5;
1 Thess 5:1–6; Matt 25:14–30

USE IT OR LOSE IT!

One is amazed by the results of an Internet search for the phrase "use it or lose it." The listing is easily a seven-figure number. A good portion of this listing deals with issues such as free speech, brain function, and muscle tone, to name but a few. These are excellent examples, for it is easy to see in such situations that if you don't use it, you certainly will lose it.

Today's Gospel offers us another example. A man went on a journey and entrusted his servants with his money. Upon his return, he required an accounting of them. A talent was about six thousand denarii, and one denarius was equivalent to a day's wage. Therefore, even the servant who received only one talent was entrusted with a sizable amount of money. Some readers have been troubled by the harshness of the master's treatment of that third man. After all, he simply did not direct the servants to invest the money. Why should one be penalized for not having done so? We can only conclude that investment was presumed. In other words: "Use it or lose it."

The readings of these last Sundays of the liturgical year prompt us to look at different aspects of the end-time. Last week we were exhorted to await that time of fulfillment in constant readiness. Today we are told that we cannot simply sit back and wait for that time to dawn. We have responsibilities; we must be industrious while we wait. The man who buried the money in the ground condemned himself with his own words, for he knew that he would be held accountable: "I knew that you were a demanding person." Thus he is punished, not because he was a poor manager of funds, but because he did not take his responsibilities seriously enough.

The sketch of the woman in the first reading depicts the complete opposite of this irresponsible man. She not only fulfilled her responsibilities, but she did so in an exceptional way. This picture of an industrious wife troubles some women who see it as merely a reinforcement of a patriarchal stereotype. It should be noted, however, that in ancient Israel's Wisdom tradition the wise person is held up as a model to be emulated. And here the ideal wise person is a woman. The character of her responsibilities is not the issue. Rather, it is her faithfulness in carrying them out. They were what her circumstances expected of her, and she was faithful.

The second reading underscores the unexpectedness of the return of the Lord. Paul insists that this event will come "like a thief in the night." He employs two other end-time themes, namely, "day of the LORD" and "birth pangs of the messiah." "Day of the LORD" is found in the prophetic writings, where it originally indicated that the Israelites looked forward to this day as a time of punishment for their enemies, but of good fortune for themselves. Amos shocked them by directing the pronouncement of punishment toward the people of both the northern and the southern kingdoms (Amos 5:18–20). Paul uses this well-known theme to assure the Thessalonians that the suffering they will inevitably endure is really end-time suffering.

In early Jewish tradition, end-time suffering was referred to as the "birth pangs of the messiah" (Isa 26:17; Matt 24:9; John 16:21; Rev 12:2). It characterized the pain one would have to endure as the new age of fulfillment was being born. Paul is here encouraging his suffering Christian converts, assuring them that their affliction is not a punishment, but is actually part of the birthing of this new age.

To what do these readings call us today? First, it is important to note that we are accountable to God, not so much for obedience to rules and regulations, but for the responsibilities of our life situations. Parents must devote themselves wholeheartedly to parenting, teachers to teaching, politicians to lawmaking, and so forth. The way we fulfill these responsibilities may be influenced by the cultural circumstances of our day, but fulfill them we must. There is no life calling that is devoid of obligations, and usually they somehow include service to others. It is in faithful accomplishment of the tasks of life that we make present the reign of God among us, that we bring to birth the age of fulfillment.

Second, fidelity to these obligations may well result in hardship. If we treat this hardship as the birth pangs accompanying the end-time, our suffering will help bring forth a new age.

Finally, though the reading from Paul and the Gospel seem to be talking about the end of all time, the final coming of Jesus at the end of time, they are meant to summon us to end-time living. Such living demonstrates that Jesus has indeed already come. In this way, every day becomes an end-time day for us.

Praying with Scripture

- Pray for the courage to endure the hardship that fidelity to God's plan might entail.

- What can you do to make everyday an end-time day?

- How faithful are you to the responsibilities of your life situation?

THIRTY-FOURTH SUNDAY IN ORDINARY TIME
OUR LORD JESUS CHRIST THE KING
Readings:
Ezek 34:11–12, 15–17; Ps 23:1–3, 5–6;
1 Cor 15:20–26, 28; Matt 25:31–46

LET ALL BE AT PEACE!

"Let all be at peace!" This phrase from the Rule of St. Benedict envisions a situation in which all members of the community are free of anxiety, receiving what they need. This understanding of peace corresponds with the biblical concept referred to on the Thirty-second Sunday, namely, a life that includes everything people need to be happy and to thrive. To live in such a community, in such a world, is the dream of every woman and man. The readings for today show that it is God's dream for us as well.

On this last Sunday of the liturgical year, the readings offer us a montage of images and themes. The first reading paints a picture of pastoral tranquility, the hues of which are deepened by a similar scene in the psalm response. The reading from Corinthians heralds the victory of Jesus, which was bought at a great price. The Gospel depicts Matthew's impression of the final judgment. Finally, all of these themes and images come together within the context of the feast of Christ the King. But what are we to make of all these themes, some of which appear to be in conflict with others? The feast determines the overarching theme, which is prominent in the first reading. There we find the picture of peace that is at the heart of end-time expectation. The source of that peace is the care and solicitude of the shepherd. Ezekiel states that this shepherd is none other than God: "I myself will look after and tend my sheep." This characterization of the divine is reiterated in the psalm response: "The LORD is my shepherd; I shall not want."

Chosen for the feast of Christ the King, these readings take on christological significance. It is Jesus who rules over us just as a shepherd lovingly tends the sheep. Our king is a personal protector and provider, not an impersonal authority. He is particularly attentive to those who are needy, those who are injured or sick, and those who have strayed. Though he does "judge between one sheep and another," it is as a caring shepherd that he does this.

The reading from Corinthians alerts us to the price our shepherd was willing to pay for the peace that has been prepared for us. He preserved us from the "cloudy and dark" dangers by taking them on himself. It was through his death and resurrection that he triumphed. However, his sovereign rule is not oppressive; quite the opposite: "In Christ shall all be brought to life."

Many people find the tone of the Gospel rather somber. While it picks up the idea of separating sheep found in the first reading, it clearly identifies this separating as judgment, and it is the theme of judgment that sets the somber tone. Within the context of the feast and the theological sense of the other readings, however, we might read this passage in a slightly different light. Here it is the Son of Man who is characterized as the shepherd who "separates the sheep from the goats." There is an added note. We are told the reason for the judgment: "Whatever you did for the least brothers [and sisters] of mine, you did for me." This very important condition readjusts the focus of the reading from one of harsh judgment by the shepherd to one of the social responsibility of all members of the flock.

In the first reading we see the shepherd particularly attentive to the injured or sick and to those who have strayed. In the Gospel we discover that such loving attention is the responsibility of everyone ("all the nations"). Furthermore: "Whatever you did...you did for me." Jesus identifies himself with the needy, with those who are hungry or ill or naked or strangers, even those who are in prison.

This king reigns over all who have been beaten down by life, who may even have given up the struggle. He tells us that when we find such people, we must pick them up and give them food and drink and shelter and clothing and, most of all, hope. And if we fail to do this, we will suffer the consequence. The punishment of which the Gospel speaks is not suddenly sprung on people. They choose a way of living that leads to it. Women and men of goodwill everywhere know that they should care for the needy. Driven by selfishness, these people chose not to.

The Sunday that closes the liturgical year leaves us with a challenge. We should see that all members of the community are free of anxiety, receiving what they need. But it also leaves us with the assurance that the king we celebrate today rules with gentleness and care and has one wish for us all: Let all be at peace!

Praying with Scripture

- Make Psalm 23 your prayer today.

- In what ways does your life further the peace of God's reign on earth?

- What can you do today to relieve the anxiety of someone in your life?

Solemnities and Feasts

PRESENTATION OF THE LORD (FEAST)
Readings:
Mal 3:1–4; Ps 24:7–10; Heb 2:14–18; Luke 2:22–40

SING AND DANCE—OR CRY?

The readings for today's feast can confuse us. The feast itself invites us to sing and dance and celebrate the presentation of Jesus in the Temple, but some of the themes in the readings may make us want to cry. This feast brings us back to Christmas. Here we behold the proud parents bringing their newborn son to the Temple, there to be dedicated to God. During this festive event, however, the young mother is told that in the future her now helpless child will face opposition, and her own heart will be pierced with a sword. The joy of Christmas is challenged by the darkness of the crucifixion. Perhaps the feast is meant to serve as a kind of reality check, lest we linger too long in the euphoria of the nativity and forget that the child came to establish the reign of God, a reign that would not be cheerily accepted by everyone.

The principal message of the Gospel is anything but bleak. Simeon, who was "awaiting the consolation of Israel," was ecstatic when he saw the child, recognizing him as "a light for revelation to the Gentiles, and glory for your people Israel." Both he and the elderly prophetess Anna realized that "the redemption of Israel" was at hand. Little did Mary and Joseph expect that the familiar Jewish observance of dedicating the firstborn son to God would result in an extraordinary proclamation of universal salvation.

The Temple played a pivotal role in the life of Jesus. It was not merely the central Jewish shrine where sacrifice was offered and feasts were celebrated; it was revered as the sacred dwelling place of God on earth. It had been built on the *axis mundi*, the center of the world, that spot where heaven, earth, and the netherworld somehow intersected. In ancient religions, the coming of God to the temple was always a time of great anticipation and excitement. The other people in the Temple when Mary and Joseph brought the child to be dedicated may have seen just another peasant couple fulfilling an ancient religious prescription. However, the true identity of this child was revealed to Anna and Simeon. They knew that the Lord had indeed entered his Temple.

The reading from the prophet Malachi also speaks of God's coming to the Temple. There, however, God comes to purify it, not to rejoice in it or to bless it. The reference to the "day of the Lord" calls to mind warnings of earlier prophets, particularly Amos (5:18–20). Israel seems to have presumed that God's coming would be a day of blessing. Amos gave them notice that their unfaithfulness would make it a day of darkness and gloom. Today we see that the distress that they would have to endure would not be simple punishment; rather, it would be purification. Divine fury might blaze against them, but it would be the "refiner's fire" or "fuller's lye" that would refine and purify the people "like gold or like silver." And when their purification was completed, they would be fit to "offer due sacrifice to the Lord."

The author of the Letter to the Hebrews was well aware of human frailty. In the passage assigned as today's second reading, he states that Jesus' sacrifice of himself expiated the sins of the people. Though these few verses do not mention the Temple, the cultic character of the entire letter is undeniable. The sacrifice that Jesus offered, the cultic sacrifice par excellence, was associated with the Temple, either actually or theologically.

The universality of salvation spoken of in the gospel passage cannot be overlooked. Simeon declared that salvation is "prepared in the sight of all the peoples," and that it is "a light of revelation to the Gentiles" as well as "glory for your people Israel." The recognition of the child by Simeon and Anna, faithful Israelites, and their declaration of God's universal concern link this event in the life of Jesus with the Epiphany episode. In both accounts, the child is seen as the agent through whom God reaches out to the entire world. At our own time in history, the feast of the Epiphany officially closes the Christmas season. Traditionally, however, the feast of the Presentation was commemorated as the fortieth and last day of Christmas.

The responsorial psalm gathers together several themes. It invokes the sight of a procession of believers approaching the gates of the city. In the manner of antiphonal singing, they call upon those in charge to lift up the gates so that the divine king can enter his holy place. The imagery of the psalm implies that this king has been victorious over the enemies of the people. Whether these were historical enemies or spiritual foes is irrelevant, for the fundamental import of the psalm is seen in the splendor of God's approach to the Temple, an approach that brings salvation.

Praying with Scripture

- Do liturgical ceremonies open you to the power of God's love? Or are they simply rituals to be performed?

- What are the "temples" within which you meet God?

- Open your heart, your inner temple, at least once this week to someone outside of your circle of family and friends.

MOST HOLY TRINITY
Readings:
Exod 34:4b–6, 8–9; Dan 3:52–55;
2 Cor 13:11–13; John 3:16–18

THE GOD OF LOVE AND PEACE

"The grace of the Lord Jesus Christ, the love of God, and the fellowship [or community, *koinonía*] of the Holy Spirit be with all of you." This passage, taken from Paul's Second Letter to the Corinthians, is familiar to many of us, for it is often used as the greeting in our liturgy. If we look at it carefully, we will see that it not only serves as a prayer, but it is also a profession of faith in our triune God. How appropriate, then, that we reflect on its meaning on this feast of the Most Holy Trinity.

The Trinity is not only a mystery that puzzles us; it is also a fascination that continues to capture our imagination. How can three persons constitute one God? St. Patrick's three-leaf clover is a clever image, but it is far from adequate. From the very earliest centuries of Christianity, theologians have painstakingly struggled to find the exact words to explain each dimension of this divine mystery. They may have succeeded with precise definitions, but these statements have not really clarified the mystery of a triune God.

The Gospel for today provides some insight into how the early Christians perceived the relationship between two of the divine persons. There we read that God sent the Son (Jesus) into the world "that the world might be saved through him." The Father-Son language implies an intimate relationship between the two. It also suggests that salvation is initiated by God and accomplished through Jesus. The real focus of the reading shifts from the nature of God in God's self to the activity of God in our lives.

The other readings for today invite us to reflect on various other aspects of this divine activity. In the passage from Exodus we are told that God reveals the divine name LORD (YHWH) to Moses. This is followed by further divine revelation. God is "a merciful and gracious God, slow to anger and rich in kindness and fidelity." Though not a definition, this might well be the best description of God found in our entire religious tradition. It may not provide us with precise philosophical concepts, but it reveals the face that God turns toward us, a face that is certainly a true likeness of God.

This passage contains three technical covenant words: *merciful*, a word that comes from the Hebrew for "womb" and suggests God's intimate attachment to us; *kindness*, sometimes translated "steadfast love," indicates the tenacity of God's commitment to us; and *fidelity*, which points to God's trustworthiness in our regard. This characterization of God appears in the Exodus story after the people have sinned against God by offering homage to the golden calf (Exod 32). Moses refers to them as "a stiff-necked people." It is to such people that God shows kindness.

How important it is for us to remember this, lest we think

that God's mercy and graciousness are rewards granted those who are faithful. No! God enters into covenant with and is gracious and merciful toward sinners, a stiff-necked people like you and me. "The grace of the Lord Jesus Christ," of which Paul speaks, is given to those who do not deserve it; "the love of God" is showered on sinners; "the fellowship [community] of the Holy Spirit" is granted to those who are unworthy. It is the mystery of such unbounded generosity that we celebrate on this feast of the Most Holy Trinity.

The challenge of faith placed before us by this feast is not one of comprehension, for try as we might, we will never really understand the mystery of the Trinity. Rather, it is a challenge of acceptance. We are invited to believe in God's tender working in our lives, and such conviction should prompt us to live out fully that faith.

This is more a day for humble gratitude and renewed commitment than for theological speculation, as important as such speculation may be. As we reflect on God's goodness in our lives, we will begin to appreciate Moses' response. The mystery of God's goodness overwhelmed him and he "bowed down to the ground in worship." We have all been touched by God's grace, God's love, and God's fellowship (community), and so we all have much for which to be grateful. This is a day to set aside to praise God, who is described in the responsorial psalm as almighty in the heavens, but whose glory is best known to us in the blessings we experience in our own lives.

This feast also calls us to commit ourselves to communion with one another. Once again it is Paul who shows us what this means: "Mend your ways, encourage one another, agree with one another, live in peace." The Most Holy Trinity is the perfect example of unity in diversity. We most resemble this God when we live in loving harmony with each other.

Praying with Scripture

- Spend some time reflecting on God's mercy in your life.

- Make an effort to appreciate those with whom you share some form of community.

- Renew your baptismal vows and recommit yourself to the Holy Trinity.

MOST HOLY BODY AND BLOOD OF CHRIST
Readings:
Deut 8:2–3, 14b–16a; Ps 147:12–15, 19–20;
1 Cor 10:16–17; John 6:51–58

BREAD OF LIFE

I have always found the aroma of bread freshly baked very comforting. That smell always makes me feel somehow at home. Perhaps it is because bread is such a staple of life. Furthermore, it is difficult to limit oneself to a single piece of bread that has just been taken out of the oven. It is almost as if a primal craving has been tapped and an overpowering drive unleashed.

There is another kind of craving for bread, one that stems from stark necessity rather than simple or remembered pleasure. In the very country where obesity is one of the most serious health concerns, millions of people go hungry. Most of us do not know this experience. I do not mean the uneasiness we feel when we miss a meal or two. I am talking about genuine hunger, the sensation that the body has begun to feed on itself, and we are being sapped of our energy. This is a true craving for bread.

It is to just such a longing for food that Moses refers in the first reading. He reminds the Israelites, who are about to enter the land of promise, that their ancestors knew real hunger when they were in the wilderness. Their hunger was so intense that they even pleaded to return to Egypt. Though burdened there with slavery, they at least had food to eat. Moses also reminds them that God provided for those ancestors by sending manna. Scholars tell us that what the people considered miraculous food was probably quite common in that part of the desert. Still, the nature of the food is not the point of the story. What is important is that God provided nourishment when the people could not do so themselves.

Moses clearly states that God did this "in order to show [them] that not by bread alone does one live, but by every word that comes forth from the mouth of the LORD." In other words, there is a hunger that only God can satisfy. The question must be asked: Do we ever experience that hunger? Have we ever known a primal craving for God?

I am convinced that the craving for God is more common than one might think. I believe that the frantic search for meaning or for acceptance that consumes so many people today is at the heart a search for God. Furthermore, I think that there are many people who are very much like the Jewish crowds in today's Gospel. They are good people who are not prepared to accept some of the claims made by Jesus, but are still searching for God. Jesus declared, "Whoever eats my flesh and drinks my blood has eternal life." This is a bold claim indeed. What were they supposed to make of it? What do we today make of it?

Today's readings are filled with bold claims: Moses claims that we need God's word as much as we need food; Jesus claims that we must feed on his body and blood if we would have life; Paul claims that when we partake of the one loaf, we are intimately joined to one another. We need faith to accept these claims. We may all experience genuine craving for fulfillment, but only faith can help us recognize what will satisfy that craving. Today's Sequence expresses this succinctly: "Sight has fail'd, nor thought conceives, but a dauntless faith believes."

The body and blood of the Risen Christ possess extraordinary features. When we eat ordinary food, we turn it into our own being. But when we eat his body and drink his blood, we are transformed into him. A bond is forged that not only grants us life, but also endures into eternal life. Furthermore, we are bound together with all others who partake of this food and drink. Those of us who search for meaning can, through faith, find it in the life promised with this food; those of us who search for acceptance can, through faith, find it by common sharing of this one loaf. We must remember, however, that in our Eucharist celebration this bread is a body now glorified, but that was once broken, and the drink is blood of the Risen Lord now, but blood that was once poured out. We are assured life through his death. Once again, only faith can enable us to accept what we cannot fully grasp.

At the heart of the feast that we celebrate today is the fundamental mystery of God's love for us. We have been created with a craving for God. As St. Augustine said, "Our hearts are restless, until they rest in you." While we await our final fulfillment in God, we have the body and blood of Christ to satisfy our hunger and our thirst. He is the real staple of life. Once we realize this, we will not be satisfied with anything less.

Praying with Scripture

- What are the hungers in your life? Where do you seek satisfaction?

- What can you do to ease the physical hunger of people around you?

- Use the responsorial psalm as a prayer of thanksgiving for God's goodness.

NATIVITY OF ST. JOHN THE BAPTIST (SOLEMNITY)
Readings:
Isa 49:1–6; Ps 139:1–3, 13–15; Acts 13:22–26; Luke 1:57–66, 80

I AM NOT WORTHY...

Down through the ages, depictions of John the Baptist sometimes tell us more about the artist than about the man himself. Each one tried, however, to capture the intensity of John's commitment and the starkness of his life. Interestingly, the readings for the Solemnity that commemorates his nativity do not really describe the man. The reading from Isaiah is taken from one of

Isaiah's Servant Songs; the psalm praises God for the magnificence of human creation; and the Gospel recounts John's being named. It is only in the second reading, where Paul summarizes the unfolding of God's plan of salvation, that the ministry of the adult John is mentioned. Each of the readings, however, along with the psalm response, provides us with a glimpse of some aspect of this remarkable man's character and destiny.

The Gospel recounts the naming of the newly born son of Elizabeth and Zechariah. In many cultures the act of naming a child is viewed as giving that child its identity. Some societies even believed that an unnamed child was not fully human. The circumstances surrounding this naming are, in their own way, as extraordinary as was the person himself. First, the child's name was decided in heaven, not according to custom ("call him Zechariah after his father"). Second, the very name of the herald of the Messiah produced a miracle. By insisting on the name announced by the angel (Luke 1:13), Zechariah, whose lack of faith had caused him to lose his speech, regained his speech. As a young man, John spent his days in the wilderness, the place traditionally considered a testing ground. It was there that he was strengthened in spirit for the task that was before him.

Paul seems to have known all about John, though John was dead by the time Paul experienced conversion. The few sentences in Paul's description of John capture the essence of the man's ministry and his spirit. John was the herald, the one who announced the arrival of the chosen one of God. The importance of John's role cannot be overestimated. It was his task to call the people to a baptism of repentance, to prepare them for the coming of the Messiah. The importance of his role did not blind John to his own insignificance: "I am not worthy to unfasten the sandals of his feet." The gospels tell us that John and Jesus were related through their mothers (Luke 1:36). Still, John did not trade on this familiarity. Instead, he considered himself a lowly servant.

John might well have adopted the sentiments found in today's psalm. The psalmist both extols human nature as being "fearfully, wonderfully made," and acknowledges that, as Creator, God knows even the most intimate aspect of this wondrous being. And how does the psalmist respond to these marvels? With profound humility!

The first reading is one of the beautiful poetic units referred to as the Servant Songs. In it the role of the servant is sketched. This servant will be instrumental in raising up the tribes of Jacob and restoring the survivors of Israel. However, this servant is a messianic figure, not a precursor as John was. Though some people who heard John preach thought that he might have been the Messiah, John disabused them of this idea. "I am not he!" This reading was probably chosen for today's feast because of some of the literary themes it contains, not necessarily for its theology. Chief among these themes is a divinely determined destiny; both the psalmist and John the Baptist were designated before birth to play a role in the drama of salvation. Second, both men were heralds, called by God to the ministry of proclamation.

Though John did not live long enough to see the day of salvation unfold in all its richness, he announced that it was coming. He was the herald of that day, and his birth was a concrete sign that that day was imminent. He brought the people to the threshold of the new age, but he himself never stepped over into it. The idiosyncratic character of his life caught the attention of the crowds, but he did not keep this attention upon himself. Instead, he used it to point to Jesus, who appeared so commonplace to many that he might have been overlooked had not John cried out. It was John's prophetic destiny to be the sharp-edged sword, the polished arrow. His appears to have been a thankless role, but it was not. His was the last prophetic voice that challenged the people to prepare; he was privileged to see the one that others did not see. John opened the door to the future and then stepped back so that the voice from the future might call us forth.

Praying with Scripture

- Do you realize the significance of the role that you play in God's plan of salvation?

- Pray today for newborns that their potential for greatness may enrich the entire community.

- Look to John as a model of dedicated and humble service.

SAINTS PETER AND PAUL (SOLEMNITY)

Readings:
Acts 12:1–11; Ps 34:2–9;
2 Tim 4:6–8, 17–18; Matt 16:13–19

"THE CHURCH'S [REAL] FOUNDATION IS JESUS CHRIST THE LORD"

Within the recent past, the church has been tossed to and fro in storms of controversy. Not one storm—many storms. And not in one country—in many countries. It has been the target of fierce persecution, and it has also allowed evil to contaminate it from within. Whether in circumstances of harassment or scandal, the lives of many have been diminished, their confidence undermined, and their faith tested.

Without minimizing the struggles of our current situations, we should remember that dire trials are really not new to the church. From its very beginning it has known turmoil and faced opposition. The first reading for today's feast describes one such situation. Herod had killed James, the leader of the church in Jerusalem. The author of Acts of the Apostles makes a point of telling the reader that this pleased the enemies of the early church. The support of these people prompted Herod to arrest Peter, the same Peter who earlier had denied even knowing Jesus. One cannot help but wonder to what extent political support of persecution allows it to flourish. Nor can we help but wonder whether and how the support of the church in Peter's imprisonment played any role in his release.

Despite its trials, the church has survived misunderstanding, rejection, and even persecution. In fact, history has shown that it seems to flourish even more during such trying times. This is not due to the strength and holiness of its members. Though Jesus told Peter that the church would be built upon him, a well-known hymn reminds us that "the church's [real] foundation is Jesus

Christ its Lord." He is the one who commissioned Peter; he is the one who assured the church of protection. It was Jesus who stood by Paul and gave him strength to bring the gospel to the broader world. The church may have been built on Peter the former denier, and spread by Paul the former persecutor, but it is the church of Jesus Christ, and it will endure because of his promise.

We marvel at the transformation of these previously weak human leaders. As we read in the passage from Acts of the Apostles, Peter's newfound passionate commitment to his Lord and to the fledgling church resulted in his imprisonment. The church's attachment to him is seen in their prayers offered to God on his behalf. Gone is the headstrong Peter, and in his place we find a man who is willing to be led by the "angel of the Lord." Though Peter was rescued, he would be recaptured later and ultimately put to death. That was the price of his commitment.

Paul too was jailed. He did not see his imprisonment as failure, but as the destiny that was his as a consequence of his commitment to the gospel. In fact, Paul seems to have gloried in his plight, for during his ministry he had found in the Lord the strength he needed. Now, having been "poured out like a libation," he faced death, and he knew it. Still, he was confident that God would bring him "safe to his heavenly kingdom."

Today we celebrate the fidelity of these two men, sinners like us all. Initially, they were both found wanting. When they eventually repented, they were forgiven by God and by the church. Though they were victims of persecution, their commitment to Christ and to the church made them heroes. And what was the source of their strength? We find the answer to this question in the Gospel.

Who was this Jesus whose words and deeds captured the imaginations of his followers and prompted them to commit themselves wholeheartedly to him? That is the question that Jesus himself posed: "Who do people say that the Son of Man is?" Was he the great preacher John the Baptist come back from the dead? Was he the prophet Elijah, whose return was expected before the dawning of the day of salvation? Was he one of the prophets? Why did they think that he was someone from the past rather than someone from the future? According to the gospel account, "Simon Peter said in reply, 'You are the Christ, the Son of the Living God.'" And how had he come to this realization? "Flesh and blood has not revealed this to you, but my heavenly Father."

Once again we see that the genuine insight and true strength of the church do not come solely from within its members, but ultimately from God. The church was founded on an unreliable man like Peter, and the mission to the Gentile world was entrusted to an overzealous Jew like Paul. If the gates of the netherworld could not prevail against the church during its initial turbulent years or through times of corruption or persecution, surely they will not prevail in our day.

Praying with Scripture

- How have the trials facing the church affected your faith?

- In what ways might you demonstrate genuine loyalty to the church?

- How can we recognize the authentic prophetic voices in the church today?

TRANSFIGURATION OF THE LORD (FEAST)
Readings:
*Dan 7:9–10, 13–14; Ps 97:1–2, 5–6, 9;
2 Pet 1:16–19; Matt 17:1–9*

I Wish It Would Never End!

In every life there are certain experiences that we wish would never end. Children are not the only ones who hate to see the days of vacation slip by. We cherish moments of loving family gatherings, a baby's first smile of recognition, and the look of tenderness in the eyes of another. Sunrises and sunsets, the warmth of the sun and the coolness of a breeze mesmerize us. We experience moments of religious fervor, experiences of deep prayer, times when meaningful liturgy lifts us up. There are so many genuine life experiences that we might wish would never end. Incidents such as these should give us a glimpse into the experience of Peter, James, and John as recorded in today's Gospel.

Who has not wondered what it must have been like to see Jesus transformed before your very eyes? "His face shone like the sun and his clothes became white as light." What really happened? Was Jesus unable to conceal his divine being any longer, and he simply allowed its brilliance to burst into the open? Or is this a postresurrection story read back into the life of Jesus? When and how it may have happened is less important than what it means.

The story says that the three disciples were thunderstruck by what happened to Jesus. The man that they knew, the son of a carpenter, was suddenly transformed before their eyes. Furthermore, he conversed with Moses, who represented the law, and Elijah, who represented the prophets. Since the law and the prophets constituted the heart of Jewish religion, Jesus' association with these two men placed him squarely at the heart of that tradition. Finally, and most astoundingly, a voice from heaven identified him as the beloved Son of God and directed the three to listen to him. If they ever doubted Jesus, this experience certainly must have banished any misgivings. They must have thought, "I wish it would never end."

The reading from the Letter of Peter reinforces the importance of this event. The author argues that he had not fabricated the message about Jesus he had been preaching. On the contrary, he had been an eyewitness to the event of Jesus' transfiguration, and that event had grounded him in the confidence he needed to preach the prophetic message of the gospel, a message that itself continues to shine like a lamp in the darkness.

When the event on the mountain was over, and the disciples were left with only their memories, Jesus directed them to tell no one of this experience "until the Son of Man has been raised from the dead." The heavenly vision and the identification of Jesus as Son of Man explain the choice of the first reading for this feast. There we read Daniel's description of a vision that took place in heaven. In it a mysterious being "like a Son of man" is granted by God "dominion, glory, and kingship." The authority and dominion that belong to other nations is handed over to him. Unlike other kingdoms that rise and eventually fall, his will be an everlasting kingdom, bestowed by God, not attained by means of conquest or political alliance. Finally, his dominion will be exercised on earth. The one like a Son of Man may have been in heaven when he received his commission, he may even rule from some exalted place in the heavens, but his kingdom belongs to the earth.

The themes for this feast are not all blinding in their brilliance. The account of the transfiguration ends with a reference to Jesus' death. One might wonder why, if Jesus shares in the glory and power of God, he would have to face ignominious death. Neither the Gospel nor the first reading mentions any kind of opposition. However, the second reading does speak of the dark place into which the lamp of truth can shine.

By some horrible coincidence, we celebrate the feast of the manifestation of Christ's brilliance on the day that the world marks another cosmic occurrence, the anniversary of its birth into the atomic age at Hiroshima. The paradox of these events should not be lost on us. The white light that shone from Christ was a mere suggestion of the divine splendor that is beyond human comprehension; the flashing light from the atomic explosion was an omen of the destructive force that is within human grasp. It is imperative that the horror of the latter be brought under the control of the glory of the former. The light that has emerged from human ingenuity can both enlighten and put an end to all enlightenment. It is up to us to decide in which kingdom we wish to live. Will it be the world of human power and domination? Or will we choose the reign of God and submit ourselves to the dominion of the Son of Man?

Praying with Scripture

- Are you are attracted by the mysterious power of God as much or as often as you are by the abilities of human ingenuity?

- Does the glory of the Risen Lord shine through in the way you live your life?

- Make today's psalm response your own prayer of praise.

ASSUMPTION OF THE BLESSED VIRGIN MARY (SOLEMNITY)
Readings:
Rev 11:19a, 12:1–6a, 10ab; Ps 45:19–12, 16;
1 Cor 15:20–27; Luke 1:39–56

BLESSED IS THE FRUIT OF YOUR WOMB

Many homes proudly display pictures of family members or of times and places not to be forgotten. Some of these pictures are in single frames. Others consist of two or three photos hinged together. As we celebrate this Marian feast, the church offers us two depictions of Mary. In the Western church this is the feast of her assumption; in the East it commemorates her dormition or falling asleep. It is interesting that the readings for the feast directly address neither celebration, but focus on different aspects of this remarkable woman.

The reading from Revelation paints a picture of a woman in the splendor of the cosmos, pursued by a dragon. In this mythical depiction, she gives birth to a great ruler who is ultimately caught up with God. This is a picture of brilliant colors and mesmerizing activity. One can hardly take one's eyes from it. Next to it is a picture of a peasant girl, herself with child, on a road that will take her to an older relative who is also pregnant. The scene is uneventful, almost sweet in its simplicity. It hardly compares with the first scenario.

A stranger might wonder why these two pictures are hinged. One would have to know the family to realize that the pregnant woman in each picture is important because of her unborn child. This becomes clear in the reading from Paul. The Risen Christ is the focus there, just as the child is the focal point of both of these hinged pictures. If we examine the readings closely, we will discover this.

The cosmic imagery in the first reading is startling in its extravagance, dynamism, and reversal. We first see a woman adorned in royal splendor. She cries aloud in labor as her son is born. He is caught up into heaven with God, but she flees into the desert. Though the author of Revelation may not have had Mary in mind while describing this vision, when the imagery is applied to Mary, as it is on this Marian feast, it suggests that she has a place both on earth and in heaven. Clearly her importance lies in her having brought forth the child who was "destined to rule all the nations."

The very first verse of the reading from Revelation sets the context within which the woman heavy with child should be understood. It calls to mind an ancient Israelite object that symbolized the presence of God in the midst of the people: "The ark of his covenant could be seen in the Temple." In this reading, the woman represents the ark, and the child in her womb is the "Anointed One" of God. The imagery in this passage, though rich, is also confusing. This woman "clothed with the sun, with the moon beneath her feet" is thought by some to be Mary, who brought forth the historical Jesus. He was certainly the presence of God in the midst of the people of his time. The woman has also been identified as the church, who brings forth the Risen Christ— certainly the presence of God in the midst of the people of all times. This mysterious woman, whether she is Mary or the church, brings Christ into the lives of others.

In some circles, devotion to Mary has waned over the recent past. The image of a docile wife and a stay-at-home mother who is dependent upon others for support has lost its appeal. However, the image of Mary that is offered in today's Gospel paints an entirely different picture. Though Mary was herself with child, she set aside her own comfort and journeyed to the hill country to visit and care for an older relative who would soon give birth. In this reading she is also a true Christ-bearer, one who brings Christ to others. Her prayer is reminiscent of the victory hymns of Miriam (Exod 15:1–18), Hannah (1 Sam 2:1–10), and Judith (Jdt 16:1–17). In it Mary first gives praise to God for according her a dignity that will be recognized by all. She then thanks God for having cared for the lowly and the poor, for having fed the hungry, and for having humbled the arrogant.

Paul declares that Christ is "the first fruits of those who have fallen asleep." We might say that Mary is the "second fruit." Her body was sacred, because it bore the Messiah of God, Jesus the Lord. We too are called to enter into the mystery of "life after death." "In Christ [we] shall all be brought to life, but each in proper order: Christ the first fruits; [Mary the second fruit], then, at his coming, those who belong to Christ," all those who in any way have brought Christ into the lives of others. Mary is a perfect model for us in this regard.

Praying with Scripture

- Marian devotion has decreased lately. What image of Mary might be relevant for our time?

- What about Mary most inspires you? How might you imitate this characteristic?

- Pray the Hail Mary slowly, reflecting on each word and phrase.

EXALTATION OF THE HOLY CROSS (FEAST)
Readings:
Num 21:4b–9; Ps 78:1–2, 34–38;
Phil 2:6–11; John 3:13–17

I WOULD DO ANYTHING...

"I would do anything...!" That's a phrase we hear often. It may even play an important role in our own lives. "I would do anything to have your good looks"—and some people go to great lengths to try to change their appearance. "I would do anything for your love"—and many people actually compromise themselves in order to gain affection. "I would do anything for you." Unlike the previous two examples, this expression often flows from unselfish love. True friends and lovers, parents and children are often willing to do anything for those they love. Such self-emptying love is a reflection of the unselfish love that God has toward each one of us.

This feast, the Exaltation of the Holy Cross, reminds us of the somber but hopeful rites of Good Friday. On that day we concentrated on the immense suffering that Jesus endured for us. Today, as we commemorate the finding of relics of the true cross by Helena, the mother of Emperor Constantine, we focus on the power of the cross in our lives.

Although Jesus is not quoted in the reading from Paul, behind it we can clearly hear him say, "I would do anything for you." Paul insists that this is exactly what Jesus did. He not only emptied himself of life, but he emptied himself of any divine privilege that might have preserved him from torturous suffering and shameful death. Paul further states that it was not so much because Jesus suffered and died that God exalted him, but because he was willing to empty himself, to do anything for us. "Because of this, God greatly exalted him."

We should not be surprised at Jesus' willingness to do anything for us. That seems to be the nature of our God. Creation itself is the child born of God's desire to give. And each one of us is a unique expression of that unselfish love. Besides the fundamental gift of life and the human ability self-consciously to reflect on life, we have each been generously blessed in more ways than we can image. All of these gifts cry out the love of God: "I would do anything for you."

The cross has become the ultimate symbol of God's willingness to do anything for us. Today's other readings call our attention to the healing and life-giving powers of the cross. The serpent fashioned by Moses and lifted up on the pole became the source of healing for anyone who looked upon it. These were not sinless people. The affliction from which they were healed was a punishment for their murmuring against God. God turned things upside down; the serpent that originally plagued them is now the symbol of their healing. We can see that it was out of love that God gave them another chance at life.

In the Gospel, Jesus refers to this traditional story in his instruction to Nicodemus. Jesus too will be lifted up, and anyone who looks upon him (believes in him) will have eternal life. As before, we see that God reverses the way we understand. The cross, which was a sign of shame and misery, becomes a symbol of glory and exaltation. Once again we see that God is willing to give people another chance at life. And why? Because "God so loved the world."

What does this mean for us? How might we revere the cross without making it merely a relic to be brought out for devotional veneration on stated feast days? Perhaps it would be best to focus not simply on the cross itself but on what it symbolizes, namely, God's desire to do anything for us and Jesus' willingness to empty himself for us. Once again it is the reading from Paul that provides us with the real challenge. He presents this picture of Jesus to the Christians in Philippi not simply for their edification, but for their imitation. With them, we are summoned to pattern our lives after Jesus, who emptied himself for the sake of others.

Our tradition tells us that the cross has saved us; do our lives show this? Are we any better than the people in the wilderness who murmured against God when they found themselves in a situation not to their liking? Like those smitten by serpents, are we suffering from the poison with which our world is infected? Or have we turned to God for healing? And have we become the avenue of healing for others?

The readings for this feast focus on healing and new life, which were purchased at the price of great suffering. Our societies, our families, and our church certainly need both healing and new life. And they are available to us if we look to Jesus, who, having been lifted up, is there for us as the supreme model. A model of what? A model of self-emptying love. *That* is the challenge placed before us today.

Praying with Scripture

- Ponder the many ways in which God has done everything for you. Be grateful.

- In what ways have you experienced the unselfish love of others? Be grateful.

- How might you bring the self-emptying love of God to the people whose lives touch yours in some way?

ALL SAINTS (SOLEMNITY)
Readings:
Rev 7:2–4, 9–14; Ps 24:1–6;
1 John 3:1–3; Matt 5:1–12a

WHEN THE SAINTS COME MARCHING IN!

"I want to be in that number, when the saints come marching in!" Who has not heard that rousing hymn and wanted to be part of that glorious parade? It is easy to clap one's hands to that stirring melody, but do we really want to join the parade? The fee seems so high. So often one has to go through a time of great distress, to wash one's robes in the blood of the lamb. In other words, to be a saint, be prepared to suffer. At least, according to the first reading.

But wait! Is it really suffering that makes us saints? The second reading tells us that it is God's love that transforms us into children of God. We may not always live up to this dignity, but, as children of God, we are indeed God's holy ones. Then what about suffering? It is true that sometimes when we are faithful, "the world does not know us." Society might ridicule us, reject us, or even persecute us. At such times, our own challenge to be holy and the opposition of the world explain much of the suffering we may have to face. Still, it is God's love and our response to that love, not suffering in itself, that make us saints.

The verses from the psalm include a question-answer exchange: Who is fit to approach God? We might rephrase that to ask, Who are the saints? In ancient Near Eastern mythology, the highest mountain was thought to be the dwelling place of the major god. Israel appropriated this concept, claiming that its God did indeed dwell on the highest mountain. Eventually, the hill on which the Temple was built was considered this sacred mountain. Today's psalm asks who might be worthy to climb that mountain to enter the presence of God.

Ancient Israel's laws of cultic purity are quite clear on this matter. One had to be physically whole with no handicaps, as well

183

as having observed certain cultic regulations (cf. Lev 17—20). Today's psalm response, however, offers another set of criteria for admission to the presence of God. It answers the question of who can approach God in a very different way. Here we read that it will be "One whose hands are sinless, whose heart is clean, who desires not what is vain." This means that access to God is not limited to a chosen few. Everyone can climb the mountain of God; everyone can be in that number, as the song says, as long as each one possesses the right interior dispositions.

The Beatitudes found in the gospel account remind us that the disposition needed to approach God is not equated with obedience to laws. Rather, it is brought to birth in our relationships with others. It calls us to be poor in spirit and clean of heart, to be comforting, meek, and merciful; it challenges us to hunger and thirst for righteousness and to work for peace. The saints of God are not merely those who conform to religious regulations, as high-minded as they might be. They are people who seek to alleviate the desperate plight of those who lack material means of survival, whether they are in faraway lands or in their own communities. They act as consoling brothers and sisters to those crushed by loss and fear and despair. They strive to empower rather than intimidate, to encourage rather than judge. They commit themselves to justice for all, not merely for themselves or for those with whom they agree. They extend to others the mercy that they have received from God. And when God's reign is under attack, they find the courage to stand steadfast on the side of truth and integrity, regardless of the cost that this might exact.

What enables the saints of God to live such noble, often heroic lives? It is the love of God that has been bestowed on them. Living in this way is not always easy. At times the hardest obstacle to overcome in choosing such a way of life is not persecution by the world or opposition from others, but one's own selfishness and lack of concern for others. But God's love can transform us.

We all know people who are living examples of this kind of holiness. They are the ones who stand tall in times of crisis, who step forward in times of need. They are women and men of principle, members of our families, neighbors among whom we live. There is seldom fanfare when they practice virtue, but their virtue leaves its mark on the lives of others. These are the saints we celebrate today; this is the multitude among whom we want to be numbered. In some ways, we ourselves might already shape our lives in this way. If so, then we are already "in that number." Will we accept the challenge?

Praying with Scripture

- Who are the saints in your life? What makes them holy?

- Which Beatitude holds special appeal for you? Why?

- What must you change in your life so that you can be counted "in that number"?

ALL THE FAITHFUL DEPARTED (COMMEMORATION)
Readings:
Wis 3:1–9; Ps 23:1–6; Rom 5:5–11; John 11:17–27

WHERE DO WE GO WHEN WE DIE?

Where do we go when we die? This is not a frivolous question. Nor is it a question that only the simple ask. The question of human destiny after death has puzzled people of all cultures from the beginning of time, and it continues to puzzle many today. This question in no way suggests a lack of faith; rather, it underscores some of the mystery surrounding death. We know what happens to the body, but what is the fate of that spirit-force or inner self that marks each individual as a unique person?

In the past, the commemoration of All the Faithful Departed focused our attention on our role in the deliverance of the "poor souls in purgatory." They were described as the Church Suffering, waiting for what we, the Church Militant, would do to alleviate their suffering so that they might join the saints in heaven, also known as the Church Triumphant. We said prayers on their behalf and made visits to the Blessed Sacrament in order to gain indulgences that might shorten their stay in that nebulous place of temporal punishment known as purgatory. Without denying our need to be purified of the traces of sinfulness before we can stand in the presence of the all-holy God, the readings for today (only a few among many choices available in the lectionary) suggest a very different focus for our consideration.

The passage from Wisdom is quite consoling. This is the reason why many people choose it as a reading for funerals. It states that the righteous dead are secure in the protection of God. Only the foolish think that "their going forth from us [is] utter destruction." We grieve their death; their passing is our loss. But is it *their* loss? They have hope that is "full of immortality." In other words, their hope cannot be extinguished by death. Though this book was written in Greek, its teaching about future fulfillment grows out of ancient Jewish thinking. This means that the possibility of existence after this life does not flow from the Greek notion of the immortality of the soul, but is grounded in the Hebrew concept of covenant bond. These dead are identified as "just" or righteous and "faithful." According to Hebrew thought, human righteousness comes through covenant union with God, who alone is righteous. At issue here is whether or not death will sever this bond of covenant union.

The psalm is also comforting. Here God is characterized as a gentle shepherd who leads the psalmist through the dark valley. There is no fear here, only trust and courage. The valley of "deep darkness" can be a reference to the darkest part of the terrain or to the gloom that can overwhelm an individual. However, it also has a mythological connotation, and is frequently interpreted as death. Whichever meaning is intended here, the psalmist claims to be unafraid, for the presence of the LORD is reassuring.

Paul too speaks of hope, a hope grounded in God's love. He insists that we have every reason to hope, for if Jesus died for us when we were still sinners, how much more can we expect from God now that we have been made righteous through our baptismal participation in the shedding of Jesus' blood? To be engulfed by water is to be swallowed up by chaos and death. This symbolism lent itself to Paul's describing both the death of Christ and the baptism of Christians. Christ was plunged into the chaos of death; the Christians were plunged into the death of chaos. By the power of God, Christ conquered death and rose to a new life of glory; by the power of God, the Christians participate in Christ's victory and are raised to the glory of a new life. This is certainly grounds for hope.

The point of the gospel story is really not the resurrection of Lazarus, which could prompt us to hope that we or our loved ones might be restored to life, but the claim that Jesus himself is the resurrection and the life. After all, Lazarus had to die again, but what Jesus promised was a life that is not subject to death: "Who lives and believes in me will never die." Here is that troubling word again: Believe. Do we believe that Jesus can do this? Do we believe that Jesus *will* do this? Do we believe that our beloved dead are indeed secure in the hand of God?

So, where do we go when we die? The readings for today do not tell us. But they do give us reason to hope. They assure us that the righteous dead are safe with God; that this righteousness is derived from our covenant union with God; and that the one who makes promises is himself "the resurrection and the life."

Praying with Scripture

- How often do you think about the inevitability of death?

- Reflect on the consoling words found in the first reading.

- Confidently commit yourself and your loved ones to Jesus, who is "the resurrection and the life."

DEDICATION OF THE LATERAN BASILICA (FEAST)
Readings:
Ezek 47:1–2, 8–9, 12; Ps 46:2–3, 5–6, 8–9;
2 Cor 3:9c–11, 16–17; John 2:13–22

THE CHURCH ON THE HILL

Some might wonder why we celebrate the dedication of a basilica that most of us will never visit. Is it simply because it is the "pope's church"? Or, as the "mother church" of all churches, should this basilica and this commemoration remind us that we are all children of the same church body? In a way, today is "Mother Church Day."

Many people maintain that old churches possess a transcendental quality. Their vaulted ceilings rise to heaven. Their artworks recount stories of religious history and the women and men who made it. The aroma of incense ascending to God still wafts in their rafters where faint echoes of mystic chant and polyphony may still be heard. No wonder such places were cherished; one met God there. Such churches are not merely remnants of times past. Their very structure proclaims elements of the faith we continue to profess. It would be a shame if they were lost to us.

More modern churches express other aspects of our faith. Many focus on the communal dimension of our worship. While the altar remains the focal point of attention, the sanctuary is often located within the body of the church rather than against the front wall. Thus our perspective shifts from understanding "church" exclusively as the sacred place of worship to experiencing "church" as the gathered assembly of worshipers.

In Ezekiel's vision, the Temple is depicted as the source of life-giving water that flows in all directions, providing fresh water for living creatures and enabling trees and plants to produce fruits in abundance. How reassuring this image must have been for exiled Israelites. It promised that their recently destroyed Temple would once again be their source of spiritual life.

And what of us? If the temple (church) is a metaphor for today's believing community, what might this image mean for us? Too often when we think of the church as a source of life, we limit our understanding to its doctrines or its hierarchy. But *we* are the church! You and I! That is what Paul emphatically declares today. "Brothers and sisters: *You* are the temple of God." Reading Ezekiel through Paul's understanding of church, we might say that the life-giving power of God flows through us to the rest of the world. We are the branches of the river that bring God's nourishment and healing to others; or at least we can be if we realize our magnificent calling and are willing to give of ourselves.

Paul insists, "The Spirit of God dwells in you!" We have heard this so often that it may cease to mean much to us. "The Spirit of God dwells in you." This is the same Spirit that raised Jesus from the dead (cf. Rom 8:11); the same Spirit that has come to renew the face of the earth (cf. Ps 104:30). What power of transformation dwells within us!!

There is a shadow side to today's pictures of the Temple. Ezekiel shows us what this temple (church) was meant to be—a source of life. But the reading from John warns us of what it might become—a den of thieves. Again, it is easy to limit the message of Jesus' condemnation to those today who have tarnished the church's glorious reputation. But *we* are the church! The warning is meant for all of us.

The deceptions of many church leaders have recently been brought to light. Add to these offenses our mismanagement of church funds, disputes over the rights of lay workers, and the marginalization of women, to name but a few indignities. And some of this seems to be justified by current church law. We should remember that the buying and selling of animals for sacrifice and the changing of "profane" money so that only "sacred" money would be used in Temple transactions were Temple laws intended to facilitate proper worship. Over time, however, their observance allowed abuses to creep in. Might the same be said about certain church laws today?

Our local church communities have other difficulties to face as well. Parishes with rich ethnic histories are challenged by the influx of ethnic groups who speak other languages and cherish other religious devotions. Too often differences spawn divisions. People without children sometimes resent having to provide for the religious education of parishioners they do not even know. The way parish funds are distributed can result in more division. The very people who need help may be deprived of it because of the depleted church funds. We all suffer because some have made the church a "den of thieves."

Today we celebrate a feast that reminds us of our unity as church. In the face of our sins and limitations, we declare with the psalmist, "God is our refuge and our strength." The Spirit of God dwells within us, and with that power we can indeed renew the face of the earth.

Praying with Scripture

- Do something to celebrate "Mother Church Day."

- How do you contribute to the life of your parish church?

- What might you do to remedy some of the ills of the church?

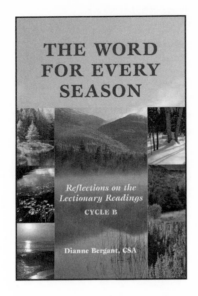

ALSO BY DIANNE BERGANT

The Word for Every Season
Reflections on the Lectionary Readings
(Cycle B)
Dianne Bergant, CSA

A well-known biblical scholar presents thought-provoking reflections on the lectionary readings for each Sunday and feast for the Year of Mark.

978-0-8091-4545-4 Paperback

The Word for Every Season
Reflections on the Lectionary Readings
(Cycle C)
Dianne Bergant, CSA

Reflections for the Year of Luke.

978-0-8091-4607-9 Paperback

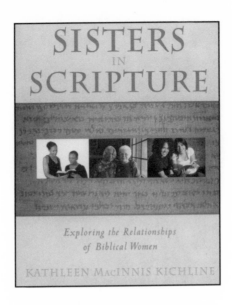

Sisters in Scripture
Exploring the Relationships of Biblical Women
Kathleen MacInnis Kichline

Uses tools of biblical scholarship, prayer, reflection and the insights of other women to explore the relationships of various women of both the Old and New Testament.

978-0-8091-4580-5 Paperback

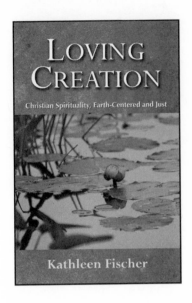

Loving Creation
Christian Spirituality, Earth-Centered and Just
Kathleen Fischer

Describes the transformation of mind and heart that is required for a new way of life on our planet, offering a holistic Christian spirituality that is both Earth-centered and justice-oriented.

978-0-8091-4603-1 Paperback

Spiritual Masters for All Seasons
Michael Ford

HiddenSpring

A blend of the spiritual and journalistic, this book explores the outer characters and inner convictions of the most inspirational figures of recent times.

978-1-58768-055-7 Paperback

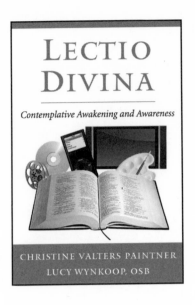

Lectio Divina
Contemplative Awakening and Awareness
Christine Valters Paintner and Lucy Wynkoop, OSB

Lectio Divina develops this ancient prayer practice as a spirituality that cultivates the ability to listen for God in the whole of life.

978-0-8091-4531-7 Paperback

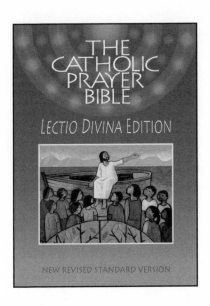

The Catholic Prayer Bible (NRSV)
Lectio Divina Edition
Paulist Press

An ideal Bible for anyone who desires to reflect on the individual stories and chapters of just one, or even all, of the biblical books, while being led to prayer though meditation on that biblical passage.

978-0-8091-0587-8 Hardcover
978-0-8091-4663-5 Paperback